W9-AVC-569

FALSE
START

FALSE START

How the New Browns
Were Set Up to Fail

Terry Pluto

GRAY & COMPANY, PUBLISHERS
Cleveland

Gray & Company, Publishers
www.grayco.com

Library of Congress Cataloging-in-Publication Data

Pluto, Terry, 1955–
False start : how the new browns were set up to fail /
by Terry Pluto.
p. cm.
ISBN 1-886228-88-4
1. Cleveland Browns (Football team : 1999) 2. Cleveland
Browns (Football team : 1946–1995) 3. Football fans—
Ohio—Cleveland—Anecdotes. I. Title.
GV956.C6P57 2004   796.332'64'0977132—dc22
2004015510

ISBN 1-886228-88-4
Printed in the United States of America
Second printing

To Browns fans:
You deserve better.

Contents

Acknowledgments

I want to thank Chris Palmer for several interviews, for opening his heart and being a man worth the admiration of every Browns fan.

I also want to thank Butch Davis and Carmen Policy for their help and their interviews.

Former Browns public relations director Todd Stewart was an enormous asset as I was putting this book together. He would be a major addition to the front office of any pro team. His assistants, Ken Mather and Amy Palcic, also were very helpful.

Kevin Byrne, formerly of the Browns and now of the Baltimore Ravens, was also very helpful.

Geoff Beckman contributed some wonderful research. Pat McManamon taught me more about pro football than anyone. It was an honor to sit next to him at games for five years.

I'm grateful to Chris Andrikanich for suggesting the title.

David Gray had faith in this project from the beginning, and Faith Hamlin is the Bernie Kosar of agents.

And thanks to all the readers who wrote me to share their own feelings about the Browns.

Acknowledgements

FALSE
START

1. Your Team Never Had a Chance

It was a fall Sunday and I had no understanding of football. I remember running into the house to ask my dad a question. He was in his sofa chair, watching the game on our Sylvania black and white TV. I was ready to run back outside when he almost begged me to watch the game with him. I vividly remember watching a player with No. 32 running and several opposing players bounced off him as he carried the football. I asked my dad, "How does he do that?" My dad said, "He keeps moving his legs." From there, my dad told me about Jim Brown and the Cleveland Browns. I was hooked. . . . My dad passed away when I was a high school senior. I will always have memories of us and our Browns. Our lying crossways across his bed listening to the Browns win the 1964 championship over the Baltimore Colts. His throwing me the football in our backyard while saying, "Frank Ryan hits Gary Collins with the touchdown pass . . . Bill Nelsen to Paul Warfield over the middle." Win or lose, they are always our Cleveland Browns.

—Martin T. Zimmer

Your team never had a chance.

Browns fans need to know that about the reincarnated franchise that returned to the National Football League in 1999.

The NFL never should have allowed Art Modell to hijack

the franchise to Baltimore. And Modell never should have even considered moving the team when he had the perfect buyer sitting right next to him in his suite on game day—a man named Al Lerner. But Modell was one of the boys, a veteran owner, and the league loves to take care of its own. And if it's unfair to the fans, so what? They'll just put an expansion team in there and make even more money in the process.

It was all about money.

Never forget that.

Money for Modell, and money for his lodge brothers in the NFL owners boxes.

(Can anyone say Personal Seat License without reaching for the Tums?)

This is the book the NFL really doesn't want you to read. It's the story of how some of the best football fans in the country were betrayed, abused, and finally stuck with an inferior product—but charged more for it. What has been the return on their investment? What have fans, who bought every ticket for every game since the Browns came back in 1999, received as a reward?

Heartaches, headaches and frustration.

That should come as no surprise. The NFL hamstrung the new Browns from the beginning, and for very selfish reasons. This led to a variety of poor decisions that haunt the franchise to this day.

Is it possible the Browns can overcome all this and even be a contender any time soon?

This is the NFL, where it seems almost any team can make the Super Bowl, unless it happens to be playing in Cleveland. So, yes, the Browns could have a playoff team in the near future. They could be a factor in the playoffs. They could finally make their fans bark for joy rather than howl in pain. But if it happens, it's because the team has overcome a ridiculous number of obstacles, most of which were put into place by a league that has dollar signs for eyes.

And that makes me mad, because Browns fans deserve better.

Who is the typical Browns fan?
It may be Dan Gilles, who sent me this letter:

I don't weigh 500 pounds and wear some ratty old dog mask to games. I don't dress in any outlandish outfits. I don't tailgate or paint my vehicle brown and orange when I go to games.

So why is he such a great Browns fan?

I love my family. I love my fiancée. I love my friends and I love the Browns. Other than my wedding day, the Browns winning the Super Bowl would probably be the greatest day of my life. I can only compare the passing of my mother as being more painful than the moving of the Browns to Baltimore. My mother and I listened to that last home game in 1995. When Casey Coleman said the Browns players were shaking the fans' hands, it dawned on me that they were finally gone. My mother and I cried together after that game. That 1995 season did more to break my heart than any woman did.

But there's more . . .

I don't have season tickets, but I went to six games in 2003. They won one. I stayed to the very end each time. It would have been more fun if they were 6-0 instead of 1-5, but I wouldn't trade it for anything. What could possibly be better than being in the stands and rooting for your favorite team?

How about a team that wins at least half of its home games?

Most Browns fans are not insane. They don't think a great game is where they can throw up on someone and set a stadium record for F-bombs. They aren't the kind who show up at stadium parking lots for the high church of the NFL at 7 A.M. and begin throwing down shots of Jack Daniels in between cans of Budweiser. They don't stagger into the stadium and make the poor soul sitting next to them miserable for three hours. The drunken slobs are not the majority.

Somewhere at my parents' house, I still have Milt Morin's autograph. He signed a card for me at a church dinner. I have an autographed picture of Lou Groza, who attended several financial seminars taught by my dad. Ernie Green lived only a few blocks away, and I used to play with his kids. These players seemed a part of the town, you ran into them as part of everyday life. They were not remote heroes on a pedestal. I miss the Kardiac Kids. I even miss all the Browns songs . . . "Bernie, Bernie" . . . "The 12 Days of a Cleveland Browns Christmas." I remember when we'd gather around the TV and watch the Browns play. If the game was blacked out, we went to my grandmother's house because she had a large outdoor antenna and could pick up the Toledo station carrying the game.

—Nancy Brucken

Browns fans are special, and have a right to see themselves as such. As a sportswriter with the *Akron Beacon Journal,* I asked fans why they follow the Browns, even now. Especially now. So many responded with their stories. I asked fans to keep it short. Some tried, but they just couldn't do it. It's hard to sum up a passionate, agonizing, exciting, distressing, decades-old love affair in only a few paragraphs. Some wrote page after page, single-spaced. Everyone seemed to have a story, their own personal Browns story. Stories of why the Browns mean so much to them. Stories of how the Browns are like a second family. Stories of love and loss, and not just on the field. It seems every Browns fan has their own story, and as I tell the story of the return of the franchise starting in 1999, we'll listen to the stories of the fans who don't own a deed to the team, but are the soul of the Browns.

I still love the Browns for the following reasons:

The memory of lying on the floor with my brothers in our family room listening as Ken Coleman described the fluid motion of Bobby Mitchell scoring in every manner possible against the Eagles.

The image of Jim Brown shedding St. Louis Cardinal tacklers on the opening highlight reel of The Quarterback Club.

My father climbing on the roof of our house to adjust the TV antenna to pick up the Toledo broadcast of the 1964 NFL Championship game against the Colts, watching Frank Ryan and Gary Collins work their post-pattern magic.

Walking into old Municipal Stadium when I was college senior, then leaving convinced I'd know that I'd made it when I became a Browns' season ticket holder.

Agonizing over the extortion that PSLs represented when the Browns returned, but still deciding I couldn't miss the opening kickoff in the new stadium against the Steelers.

Knowing that the Browns and the NFL are more than just a game, but a way of life. Win or lose, as long as I draw a breath, they will always be my team . . . my Browns.

I just completed my 22nd year as a season's ticket holder.

—David Dalsky

E-mail after e-mail came in like this, and after a while, I got mad.

Mad at Art Modell, who was such a truly mediocre owner entrusted with such a civic gem, and who sold the family jewels to Baltimore.

Mad at the NFL for allowing Modell to leave, for setting up the new Browns for failure—all in the name of greed.

Mad at the first Browns management team that squandered so many draft choices, giving former general manager Dwight Clark a job that he never should have had and putting former coach Chris Palmer in a position where he had no chance to win.

Mad at the Butch Davis regime for teasing the fans with the trip to playoffs in 2002, then falling flat on its face in 2003.

Mad because Al Lerner died too soon—though I never thought I'd see Lerner as the best man to own the Browns, the guy who really understood what an owner should do, and who was willing to spend his own money to try and do it.

Mad because the fans deserve better.

Not a Super Bowl every year . . . or even every decade.

But how about one Super Bowl? Even a loss in a Super Bowl?

At least Tribe fans have their Jose Mesa and Boston Red Sox fans have Bill Buckner.

Yes, Browns fans have The Fumble . . . The Drive . . . Red

Right 88. But all those things happened in playoff games before the Super Bowl!

If you are a veteran Browns fan, think back to 1970.

The Browns won the 1964 NFL title. They lost in Green Bay for the 1965 title. In 1968 and 1969, they lost in the playoffs, one step away from the Super Bowl.

After the success of the 1960s, wasn't there reason to believe that the team would make it to at least ONE Super Bowl in the next three decades?

But if you're a Cleveland sports fan, you're used to it.

Seventeen different NFL teams have won a Super Bowl, and the Browns have yet to play in the game.

Art Modell hijacks the franchise to Baltimore and wins a Super Bowl!

Brian Billick turns down a chance to coach the Browns, and wins a Super Bowl for Modell in Baltimore!

Ozzie Newsome should be running the Browns, instead he's in charge of the Ravens where he hired Billick away from the Browns and won the Super Bowl for Modell!

Bill Belichick, of all people, resurrects his career in New England, and wins two Super Bowls!!

Carolina was 1-15 in 2001 and two seasons later, the expansion Panthers were in the Super Bowl!!!

Are we having fun yet?

I've often wondered why the Browns have such a pull on me. The only answer is the Browns keep me close to my father, who died in 1973. He loved the Browns, and he got me to love them. I haven't talked to him in more than 30 years, but I think about him often as I watch the Browns. When I'm buoyed by a great performance, I know he'd understand the feeling. I know he'd be just as annoyed

by the running backs who dance and wide receivers who don't block. And I find myself talking to him (as I am now) about something we shared and understood together. My dad died when I was 15. So many things have changed in my life since then—it's difficult for me to know how he'd react to it all. But I know how he'd feel about hearing that his grandson loves watching the Browns with his son. That knowledge helps me connect with him after three decades.
—Adam Grossberg

What can you say about a letter like that? Or this one?

I grew up in the late 1970s and 1980s with The Drive, The Fumble and I still believe in my heart that Denver missed that last field goal . . . it was definitely WIDE!!!

Being a female and crying after all those heartbreakers may seem odd for a non-Browns fan . . . but not to those who have been through it. I sometimes wonder why I look forward to the next game each year, just to get disappointed all over again. Maybe it's because I shared those moments with my dad. We'd always get excited to watch the games together and then talk about it forever after it ended. My mother never quite understands why we put ourselves through such misery every year. . . . I look forward to more and more Browns seasons to share with my dad, because he's the one responsible for me falling in love with this team.

—Stacie Cepin

There are worse things than the Browns not making the Super Bowl, or even being embarrassed by the Steelers or Bengals. But for so many Browns fans, this isn't just their team. It's part of an extended family. The Browns are a very important part of their lives, and in many ways, the friends they make at the games mean more to them than those who happen to share the same bloodlines. It's been said that a family is a bunch of people whom you end up stuck in an elevator with. But Browns fans are different. They volunteer and pay and line up to go into that elevator, even if it seems like it's going nowhere.

In 1993, I retired from the Navy and returned to my roots in Akron for one reason, the history of sports in the area. More importantly, I wanted my four children to have the same experiences I had as a child. I now live in Detroit, but every game day, I get up at 4 a.m. and make the three-hour drive to Cleveland. I park on the lot off West 3rd Street, and meet a group of guys whom I've been friends with for more than 11 years. We share PSLs and bought them together. The lot is alive with fans who think our turn is coming, the smell of BBQ and the conversations that permeate the smoke are stronger than any 5-11 season. The Browns are our excuse for coming together, but our friendship is the glue that makes sure we keep coming together.

—Ernest Jones

Browns fans rage and scream and cry and, yes, whine a little bit. But that's a sign of hope. Anger at least means you still care enough to get mad. It means you're not ready to give up. It means the Browns still matter to so many fans despite having the worst home record in the NFL since coming back in 1999, despite a 4-10 record in the playoffs since 1970. In the darkest days of the 2003 season, a frustrated Coach Butch

Davis answered his critics by saying, "Why don't these people get a life?"

I give Davis a break on this, because he really does appreciate the fans. He was just shocked at the intensity of the criticism coming his way, and spoke purely out of emotion—just as did many of the fans.

Get a life?

The Browns are not life and death. But when they are at least respectable, they make life so much better for the fans who help pay the salaries of the millionaires on the field.

2. Betrayal

No woman ever broke my heart more than when Art
Modell did when he lied to the entire Browns Nation and
copped out to Baltimore.

—Ken Keller

Did anyone really believe Art Modell would move the
Browns?

It made no sense, at least to me.

After he announced the bolt to Baltimore, I wrote a column that began with this sentence: "I'm not sure the Browns
are going anywhere."

I even called Modell to ask if he had changed his mind.

Understand that 24 hours earlier, Modell had told me his
promise not to move the team "was now null and void." But
why wouldn't he be using Baltimore as the threat to squeeze a
new stadium out of the city? Bengals owner Mike Brown had
done the same thing only a few months earlier. He threat-
ened to move to Baltimore, which not only was putting together a terrific stadium deal, but was willing to kick in about
$30 million to help Brown pay for expenses. Cincinnati then
stepped up and gave Brown a new stadium, basically mirror-
ing the lease deal that Baltimore offered. I pictured a desperate Modell trying the same tactic. Why would a man who'd
invested 35 years in the community just throw it away?

"You have the wrong man," Modell told me. "What? I'm

going to get a deal [from Baltimore], then say that Cleveland has two days to match it? That's not my style."

When it came to business, I had no idea what *was* Modell's style—other than lousy. He was the guy who told everyone about going to five different banks to come up with the money to pay the $5 million signing bonus for wide receiver Andre Rison before the 1995 season. He seemed almost proud of it. I guess he thought it showed the fans what he was willing to do to field a winner. It told me that even the bankers knew Rison was a terrible fit for the Browns, so why didn't Modell and his head coach, Bill Belichick, know that? It told me that he was doing a horrendous job of managing his team's finances. It made me wonder why go to such extremes for a moody, troubled receiver who would never remind anyone of Browns greats Paul Warfield or Gary Collins. Rison was symbolic of those final Modell years, an overrated, overpaid player with no connection to Browns fans—and no interest in making one. He was in it strictly for the money, and fit into the Browns culture about as well as a polka band would at Laguna Beach. He was the anti-Bernie Kosar. Browns fans loved Kosar, who graduated from the University of Miami a year early to help work out a deal to play for the Browns, the favorite team of his Youngstown youth. Rison would have played in Siberia if the cash was right.

As Modell was breaking the bank for Rison and plotting his move in early November of 1995, he was 70 years old. He was jealous that the Indians and Cavaliers both received sweetheart deals for new facilities from the Gateway Corporation. He may not have said so, but he probably was angry that Tribe owner Dick Jacobs was able to get his stadium built first.

"They do all this rhapsodizing about the Indians," Modell

told me. "I mean, they deserve it for what they've done lately, but for a long time, we've had a much better record and more success than they did."

Remember, this was November of 1995. The Indians had just been to the World Series. They were selling out as fans fell in love with a team that was 100-44 and loaded with stars. Meanwhile, Modell had one winning record in the 1990s and a coach in Bill Belichick who was despised by many Browns fans. In 1994, when Belichick was leading the Browns to the playoffs, countless fans told me, "I never thought I'd say this, but I'm pulling against them. I just want them to lose so they can get a new coach."

Modell didn't understand the public relations disaster he created with the hiring of Belichick. The coach was 38 at the time and not prepared for the job of running the entire football franchise. He was either "painfully shy" or "arrogant," depending upon who was talking. Over and over, Modell used the "painfully shy" line on me. The fans went in the other direction. But the real problem was Belichick's total disregard of Browns history. Combine that with his horrendous press conferences, which not only turned off the media, but gave a poor impression to the fans.

During all this, Modell was insisting, "Bill Belichick will be my last coach."

With the Browns, Belichick was the coach who rudely cut Bernie Kosar at midseason even though Vinny Testaverde was injured, and the Browns had to play third-stringer Todd Philcox. Then Belichick tried to tell the fans that he believed Philcox was a better player, which just proves bright guys (which includes Belichick) can say some very dumb things.

Why pick at this old wound?

To understand a little of where the Browns are today, fans

need to realize that Modell picked the right coach (Belichick), but not at the right time. Belichick was too young and inexperienced to turn around the Browns.

Why did Belichick become a successful coach in New England?

Because he is a bright guy. Stubborn, but smart. After being fired by Modell—guess what, he wasn't Art's "last coach"—Belichick went back to work as a defensive coordinator for his former head coach Bill Parcells. He spent five more years as an assistant, then took over the Patriots at the age of 48. He had been humbled. He figured out that just being civil in press conferences and with his players would help him be a more effective coach. Cleveland turned out to be a place where Belichick made his mistakes, where he was like a little kid learning how to ride a bike on training wheels. He wasn't ready to ride all by himself in the traffic. Now he's the Lance Armstrong of coaches, the guy at the head of the pack. If you're a true Browns fan, there is only one response to Belichick's recent success: That figures!

Meanwhile, Modell just was bitter.

He was envious of Cleveland Cavaliers owner Gordon Gund, who was romanced by the nonprofit Gateway Economic Development Corporation to move his team from Richfield Coliseum in Summit County to downtown Cleveland. It appeared everyone was getting theirs, except Art . . . at least, that's how it seemed to Modell.

"They've been telling me to wait for six years," Modell told me that night. "It's been 21 years since I took over the stadium. I feel like I've been misled."

Let's look at the records for 1990-94: 3-13, 6-10, 7-9, 7-9, and 11-5.

Is there any wonder that the public was not embracing

Modell's plea for a new stadium? All the losing. Cutting Kosar. Belichick mumbling and grimacing. Some of us in the
media called him Bitter Beer Face, not because he drank, but
due to a commercial where a guy looks like he just chugged
a quart of Valvoline. From 1990 to '94, the Browns averaged
slightly more than 70,000 fans in a crumbling stadium to see
a mediocre team with an owner who admits he had a major
money crisis. To put it in another context, from 1986 to 1994,
the Browns ranked between second and seventh in total attendance, playing to about 93 percent capacity. From 1990
to '94, with a record of 34-46, the team ranked between fifth
and seventh in attendance, playing to 89 percent capacity.

How dare the man even consider moving?

At least, that was my thought.

Could the city have handled the Browns situation better?
Of course.

Could Modell have been more politically astute? Could he
have done a better job of lobbying for a new stadium? Did
he willingly take on the old stadium as his personal beast
of burden, and then complain when it was too heavy? Does
anyone remember how in 1989, Modell's plan was to reno-
vate the old stadium so that the Browns and Indians would
both continue to play there, and Modell would remain as the
landlord for both teams? Can we consider that might have
taken him out of the first round of the Gateway development
plan? Can we just say that when it comes to the business side
of the Browns, Modell just didn't get it?

And the fans just kept loving his team.

Even when they were screaming and complaining and
demanding that Belichick be fired, they still loved the team.
Sometimes, anger is a sign of love, of hope, of wanting to be
heard and for things to change so the relationship can re-

main alive. The real danger zone for any pro team is apathy. In the pre-LeBron James days of the Cavaliers, from the middle 1990s to 2003, I wrote newspaper stories about the team and seldom received even a single e-mail. People just didn't even care enough to criticize the team. When I did hear from fans, it was that they missed the old Miracle of Richfield in 1975, or the Mark Price/Brad Daugherty/Larry Nance/Hot Rod Williams/Craig Ehlo/Lenny Wilkens era of the late 1980s and early 1990s. Occasionally, a fan wrote that if the team left town, no one would notice because it seemed as if they had been gone for years.

It was never like that with the Browns.

The ultimate testimony to the fans is what the team drew after the move was announced. Here are the crowds for the final four home games: 57,881 . . . 55,388 . . . 67,269 . . . 55,875.

Those were bodies in the seats, not tickets sold. If any sports situation pleaded for a fan boycott, this was it. But Browns fans can never really stay away from their team. I find this remarkable, because I doubt I would have attended any of those games as a fan. I was there because I was paid to write about it. Who wants to see a lame-duck team with a sullen coach and an owner who just sold out the town? But those orange helmets had such power over Browns fans, many thought they just had to be there. Maybe it was like going to a funeral, time to pay respects to someone who may have faltered late in life but still was special to you, still part of the family.

For that first home game after the move was announced, fans carried signs shaped like tombstones such as:

KOSAR #19, GONE BEFORE HIS TIME

MOVE MODELL

$PINELESS $LUG

They cheered for longtime Browns such as Tony Jones, Earnest Byner, Rob Burnett, and even Vinny Testaverde. When Belichick benched Testaverde in favor of Eric Zeier for a few games, suddenly fans thought Vinny was getting a raw deal—and they forgave him for replacing Kosar and saw him as another victim of Belichick!

This was a very strange time to be a Browns fan.

> I remember going to the very last home game prior to the team leaving for Baltimore. It was typical Northeast Ohio weather, raining one minute then freezing the next and snow soon to follow. People were pulling out sections of seats and walking out with them. . . . I have left Municipal Stadium after many losses, but this day was different. Not only were we cold and disappointed after another loss, it was as if we didn't know if we'd ever experience Browns football again. It was so empty. Not the stadium, but the feeling we had. It wasn't losing the game, but losing our team.
>
> —Todd Hittle

Here's another weird aspect to that December 12, 1995 game . . . the Browns actually won! Beat Cincinnati, 26-10. Byner, Jones, Testaverde, and others jumped into the Dawg Pound, where they were embraced by fans.

But it's hard to remember that part.

"When your heart is hurt, your head don't work right." That's a line from my friend, Bishop Joey Johnson from Akron's House of the Lord. It certainly applied on that day for Todd Hittle and his 55,874 fellow mourners. It was as if they lost, because after the game, the place was a tomb. But you could hear the echo of pounding and crashing as fans had brought screwdrivers and hammers to the game and were removing chairs, carrying them on their shoulders, out of the stadium.

In Ozzie Newsome's office in Baltimore, he has some dirt from the field from that last game. Everybody there wanted to keep some piece of the Browns.

In 1995, I wrote, "If there ever was a worse day in the history of Cleveland sports, who wants to see it? This stadium which had seen everyone from Paul Brown to Jim Brown . . . from Frank Ryan to Brian Sipe to Bernie Kosar . . . the old building seemed to just hang its head."

I look back at the final Modell years and marvel at the support:

They averaged 71,059 fans in 1993, the year they cut Kosar.

They averaged 71,012 in 1990, the year they were 3-13.

They sold more than 600 tickets to the next game within 24 hours of the move being announced.

Modell could try to argue that he didn't receive the best corporate support. He certainly had some legitimate issues with the city.

But with the fans?

They just kept coming.

This wasn't a no-fault divorce where everyone just agreed to stay friends. It was abandonment, pure and simple. It did more than take one football team out of town, it set back the franchise that was brought in to replace it.

3. Why Didn't Art Just Sell to Al?

The first time my son saw me cry was the day Art Modell stood on stage in Baltimore with the governor of Maryland to confirm the move of the Browns. My son was confused by my emotions. I told him, "You'll understand someday." My father and I developed a bond of communication through the Browns. When we had nothing to say, or wouldn't dare say it, we could always talk about the Browns. I took my father and my two sons to the final home game. At the game's end, as the Browns' players hugged fans in the Dawg Pound, I held my father and my sons close to me. It was my last opportunity to share the Browns with them.

—Dan Rudolph

Why didn't Art Modell just sell the team to Al Lerner?

That question has always bothered me, and very few in the media bothered to ask. Just think how so many lives would be different. The Browns never would have left. Ozzie Newsome could be the general manager. The team would have been bankrolled by a billionaire.

And dare I say it?

The Browns—not the Ravens—would have won a Super Bowl.

Don't think so?

If Newsome could put together a Super Bowl winner with

Modell's limited budget in Baltimore, just imagine what could have happened with Lerner's unlimited checkbook here. Sorry, didn't mean to ruin your day with all this, but it's worth considering.

All Modell had to do was sell to Lerner, who once was his best friend.

Several years ago, I asked Lerner that question.

It came after a press conference not long after he had taken over as owner of the new Browns. I had been a severe critic of him during the move, then the bidding process. I was in the "Anyone But Al" camp, because I thought his role in Modell's taking the team to Baltimore should have prevented him from being owner of the new team—just on general principle.

But Lerner prevailed.

He came up to me and said, "So this is how it's going to be?"

"How what is going to be?" I asked.

"Just tell me, are you're going to rip me all the time, or what?" he said.

"Al, you've got the team, it's over, I've had my say," I said.

"I don't understand your problem," he said.

"I don't understand why you helped Art go to Baltimore," I said. "Both of you guys had a life here, real roots. I don't get it."

"I was helping a friend,' he said.

"There had to be a better way to do it," I said.

"Art had money trouble," he said. "He needed a new stadium. He wanted to keep the team for his family. Baltimore was a way to do that."

"Why not just buy the team?" I asked. "Make him President Emeritus or something."

"He wouldn't sell it to anyone," said Lerner. "He was going to keep it."

Lerner then went into a long explanation about why he did what he did, and how anyone who was a true friend would have done the same thing. He saw the needs of helping a friend as being above every other consideration. I mentioned how important the Browns were to the community, how the fans did nothing to deserve having the team stolen. He just went back to Modell and his friendship.

We finally agreed to disagree.

Lerner also was unhappy because I had written that he bought the new Browns "to get his honor back."

I didn't realize that this was such a hot button, because as an ex-Marine, honor is up there with God, country, and family. He kept saying the honorable thing was to stick by a friend in need. The irony was that at this point, Modell and Lerner no longer were friends. They weren't even speaking.

Why was that?

"Because Art left, and Al stayed," former Browns president Carmen Policy recently told me.

Didn't Modell figure that would happen? Hey, he was leaving town on Lerner's jet. No one put a gun to Modell's head and told him to move to Baltimore. No one forced Lerner to take such an active part in the move. Both men had choices, and they made decisions that they clearly thought were best . . . for them.

As for the fans, you decide . . .

"Art could not tolerate selling the team to Al," said Policy. "They did talk about selling it to a stranger, who could keep it in town. But Art wouldn't do that, either. In the end, Art couldn't see anyone but himself owning the Browns. He knew if he moved the team, it would help him financially, and maybe he could get another shot at a Super Bowl—which is what he wanted."

Understand that Policy respects Lerner probably as much as any man. Lerner gave Policy a terrific financial deal—10 percent of the team—to join him in securing the franchise from the NFL and then setting up the first front office. Policy is not exactly unbiased. But I talked to Modell during the time of the move, and I agree with Policy. The Browns were his, and Modell was not about to give them up, period. He didn't care what he did to the fans, or what his reputation in Cleveland would become. At least not enough to do the right thing and sell to a local owner, such as his friend Al Lerner. Modell wanted to keep the Browns at any cost.

And the ones who really paid for it are you—the fans.

Just as guilty as Modell in this story is the NFL.

Consider what Modell really intended to do. He and the Baltimore Ravens now make much of the fact that Modell left the team name and colors in Cleveland. I checked the papers from November 1995, when the move was announced. There are stories that he indeed intended to call the team the Baltimore Browns. There was a story in the November 8, 1995, *Plain Dealer* under the headline: "As Modell Goes, So Goes the Name . . . City Loses Browns Nickname with Team."

Or how about this?

There was discussion in Baltimore about naming the new stadium Browns Field.

Want more?

On November 7, 1995, Modell told the *Baltimore Sun*: "I will say right now, I'm certain Bill Belichick will coach this team next year. I'm a great believer in continuity. I think he's done a good job."

Modell planned to take everything he could with him

to Baltimore. It was only after former Cleveland mayor Michael White and angry fans began demanding "Our colors, Our name, Our team!" that Modell relented as an attempt to take some of the heat off himself. Just as he called the move to Baltimore "a business decision," so was the giving of the colors and name to a Cleveland franchise to be revived later. Several of Modell's NFL friends also told him to make that gesture as some sort of peace offering to the Cleveland fans. Before I began the research for this book, I thought perhaps it wouldn't be as ugly as the first time around. I thought that time might have softened my anger, that perhaps it wasn't as outrageous and unsavory as it seemed. But it's the same rotten deal for the fans. Modell's ego would not allow him to do the right thing. Lerner's sense of friendship may be admirable to some, but helping Modell put together the Baltimore deal was not in the best interest of the Browns fans.

Nor did the NFL grant Cleveland any special favors, regardless of how that is now painted. Before Modell could move, the NFL had to approve it. They knew it was wrong. They knew Cleveland was a great football town. They knew with every beat of their heart that this was being done not for the good of the NFL or because the fans had somehow let down the Browns. It was a 70-year-old owner who couldn't balance his books, despite the league's superb revenue-sharing system. He needed to be bailed out. Modell had been in the league for 35 years, and most of the owners knew it was time for him to sell, that he had been in poor health, and that someone such as Al Lerner would be the natural successor to Modell in Cleveland. But Art wouldn't sell to anyone. He played the loyalty and sympathy card with fellow owners, reminding them of how he had been on their side of various issues over the decades.

At the same time, the NFL was cutting a separate deal with Cleveland to bring an expansion team to town in 1999, assuming a new stadium was built. But something else was being whispered in the room: "Hey, if we don't get a new stadium in OUR town, we can always threaten to move to Cleveland." Some of these guys didn't get to be millionaires by accident. They realized that having Cleveland as an open market with a new stadium on the way could be very useful to them. So many franchises either got new stadiums or better leases out of their cities because of the possibility of a move first to Baltimore—and then, once Modell grabbed that offer—relocating to Cleveland. In his excellent book on the Browns move, *Glory for Sale*, Baltimore reporter Jon Morgan wrote, "Directly or indirectly, the Browns relocation caused stadiums to be built for the Ravens, the Redskins, the Bengals, the Browns, the Bucs, the Lions, and the Seahawks. The impact of the Browns move on taxpayers nationally was staggering."

Know why else the owners went along with Modell?

They had allowed the Cardinals to move from St. Louis to Arizona . . . and the Rams to move from Los Angeles to St. Louis . . . and the Raiders to keep moving between Oakland and Anaheim . . . so why not let Art go to Baltimore, and take care of one of our own? Who knows, one day we may want to move somewhere, and we can always use support from Art Modell.

In the end, the owners voted 25-2 to back Modell. Three teams abstained: Arizona, St. Louis, and Oakland. Only two were against Modell: Buffalo's Ralph Wilson and Pittsburgh's Dan Rooney.

When the vote was over, Oakland owner Al Davis held his own mini-press conference and said, "[Modell] is the one who spoke out adamantly against [moving] the Rams. He put a lot of obstacles in our [the Raiders] way in Los Angeles, and it's déjà vu. Here he is standing up, changing everything he has said over 15 years in about one month."

So true.

4. The Big Squeeze

> The passion of being a Browns fan and the anguish that
> goes with it are worn by us like a badge of honor. We are
> dealt the firing of Paul Brown, the losing at Three Rivers
> Stadium in every way possible. There is The Drive, The
> Fumble, The Move, more years of struggling as an expansion
> team . . . and yet, we always come back for more pain and
> suffering. . . . Most of us have so many years invested
> in the Browns that we simply can't walk away even if we
> wanted to. I tried to root for another team during The Lost
> Years when the Browns didn't exist, but I couldn't.
> —Chuck Campbell

There was no conspiracy, it was just greed.

Remember that when you hear the stories about Art Modell, Al Lerner, and the Browns . . . how Lerner would help Modell move the team to Baltimore . . . the NFL would then give Lerner an expansion team . . . two cities would end up with two new stadiums. Everyone would be happy, especially the NFL, Modell, and Lerner.

I'd like to believe that scenario just because it's easy for me to think the worst of the NFL. But I know that Lerner was shocked by the backlash against him after his role in Modell's move. He never saw it coming. He should have known there would be a major public relations problem for anyone near Modell's bolt to Baltimore. I used to think that the NFL wanted Lerner to become the owner of the new Browns because he was one of the boys, a part of the league's inner circle. I was partly right. They did want Lerner. But not out of friendship. They thought he could pay the most money for the expansion franchise.

Money. Money. Money.

I wrote about that for nearly a year when covering what remains the most depressing story in my 26 years as a sportswriter—the Browns move, and the NFL's extortion plan to squeeze every dollar out of the new Browns owner. Even Lerner was surprised by their greed, and he'd known these guys for more than a decade as a minority owner of the Browns and a friend of Art Modell.

"Al thought the league should set a price for the team, then identify which groups could pay it—and from that, pick whom they thought would make the best owner," Carmen Policy told me.

The NFL thought the best owner was the one willing to pay the most. They didn't care if the guy had Cleveland roots, or if he came from Iraq. Just bring the cash, baby.

I went to the NFL meetings in Dallas, where the league began the hustle of the Browns. Dallas owner Jerry Jones said the man who ended up with the new Browns "would own a piece of Americana!" He also compared them to the New York Yankees.

Some Browns fans thought the community should own the new team, much like the Green Bay Packers. The NFL would rather cancel the Super Bowl and give back all that TV money than allow another civic group to own a team. Now the league has laws against it. Besides, if a city owns it, how can the team threaten to move if it wants a new stadium or a better lease? A team run purely for the good of the fans? Sounds communist to these guys.

Know what price they first put on the Browns?

A BILLION DOLLARS!

"A billion is not unfair," said Alex Spanos, owner of the San Diego Chargers. "I know it's worth a billion, but I don't know if anyone will pay it."

This meeting was held at the Dallas Hyatt Airport. I walked through the lobby, talking to the owners about the Browns. I had never been around a group that seemed so self-important and had so little regard for the customers. Along with some other reporters, I was asking them about what they wanted from the new Browns owner. How would they decide between the groups bidding?

"It will go to the highest bidder," said Tampa Bucs owner Malcolm Glazer.

Spanos went on and on about all the groups being from Ohio, then added, "Realistically, the price is insignificant. The main thing is the Cleveland fans will have a team. The only question is, who will be the highest bidder?"

I was ready to scream.

All the groups were NOT from Ohio. Howard Milstein was a New Yorker who owned the New York Islanders of the National Hockey League. Another was Jeremy Jacobs, who was a New Englander who owned the NHL's Boston Bruins.

All the groups were from Ohio? Were they just oblivious, or lying? It's like these guys thought they could just say anything because they owned an NFL team, so that made them right. Their pomposity and arrogance was appalling, even by the bloated standards of pro sports.

Even Al Lerner, who knew these guys, had trouble dealing with it.

Before he was granted the franchise, Lerner said, "In hindsight, the owners will see a number [bid] they like best and decide that person was brilliant."

So true.

Something else: If the price was "insignificant," then why was the bottom line the highest bidder?

As I wrote on July 28, 1998, "What if the highest bidder turns out to be an idiot?"

Obviously, the NFL didn't care.

Here's why they wanted $1 billion:

- Each franchise (except Modell's) was going to split up the expansion fee. Every team would receive 1/30th of the price. For a billion bucks, each team would get $34 million. At $500 million, it would be $17 million. Big difference.
- The higher the price for the Browns, the more it inflated the value of their own franchises.
- In 1993, the NFL charged Jacksonville and Carolina $140 million each to join the league. Five years later, they were asking for a billion? They figured it would be a minimum of $500 million.
- The league said each team would receive about $70 million a year in TV revenue, so why not ask for a billion?
- Browns fans were so excited about any team coming to town, they had bought more than 50,000 season tickets and leased 90 of the 116 luxury suites by the summer of 1998. That was with the new stadium not complete and no coach or player or front office in place for a team that was to start play in the fall of 1999.

If the NFL had even one drop of compassionate blood for Browns fans, the league would have picked an owner at that meeting in July of 1998—especially since it knew that Lerner was its man. That would have at least given the new owners about 15 months to put together a team before the first game. But no, these guys were determined to drag it out for a few more months, and drive up the price. Besides, every time a new group applied, they had to submit $150,000 just to be considered. It may sound like pocket change in the billion-dollar world of the NFL, but you had a feeling some of these guys would roll up their sleeves and stick their hands into a public toilet if they spotted a nickel at the bottom.

Now it's obvious that the league favored Lerner almost from the moment Modell moved. And the reason also is obvious: He had the biggest bankroll, worth $2.5 billion. He also was a guy whom they knew and believed would make a good business partner. He understood the game. Not on the field, but in the backrooms and boardrooms. For this reason, I'm not going to get into a debate about all the other ownership groups and their merits. In retrospect, Lerner was the best man. But not just because he had the most money. He also had the right attitude and ego for the job, along with that available stash of cash and tremendous connections with the Cleveland business and political structure. He was a guy who got things done.

That could have been determined at the first meeting in July, and it would have given the Browns a few more months to prepare for the 1999 season. Would it have made a difference? Who knows? Maybe everything would have been the same. Maybe Dwight Clark would still have been the general manager, Chris Palmer the coach, and the drafting and scouting situation a mess. Browns fans deserved better. They were entitled to their team and new front office having plenty of time—say 18 months, at least—to be in place before the first game.

But the NFL didn't care about that . . . or you!

Lerner sensed the situation was not right and would lead to problems.

"We were clearly the best group, but we almost walked away from the bidding," Carmen Policy told me. "Al kept saying it shouldn't be about just getting the highest bidder, but the best owner. But the NFL was basically saying, 'We want the best ownership group, and by the way, you also have to pay the most money.' That bothered Al."

Policy was confident they'd end up with the team. He also believed it would be a great investment, regardless of the final cost.

He kept telling Lerner, "This is the way the NFL works. But Al, once you're in, you're in. Within three weeks of getting the team, the price you paid will be meaningless except for accounting and tax purposes. The value of the franchise will increase, but more importantly, you'll get caught up in it. This is an emotional narcotic. The idea that you can do without it after you taste it—that's just not acceptable."

It's hard to believe Lerner was serious about withdrawing.

Frustrated?

Of course.

But he was a competitive man, and he certainly didn't want to lose out for one of the biggest, most public business deals in Cleveland history to Larry and Charles Dolan, Dick Jacobs, Howard Milstein, or anyone else. He also had enough exposure to the NFL and the Browns through his association with Modell to know that Policy was right. You do get hooked on the games, the season, the action, and the pressure of winning and losing. No other business quite matches it.

Policy had met Lerner only once before becoming a part of Lerner's group. In fact, Policy didn't even recall the meeting, it was brief and Lerner was with Modell. Policy was put in contact with Lerner by Dennis Swanson, president of ABC Sports. Policy was trying to help his daughter find a job in the TV business. Swanson was a friend of Lerner's. Swanson told Lerner to go after the Browns, and he mentioned that Policy was having a difficult time in San Francisco, where the 49ers ownership situation was in flux. Swanson suggested to Lerner that he recruit Policy. He then told Policy, "You need to call Al Lerner. There is no better place to be for football than Cleveland. California can slide into the ocean and Arizona can become beachfront property, but they still will be talking football in Cleveland."

Policy knew Lerner had money and clout with the NFL.

"Not only that, but I was aware—like most NFL people—that this Al Lerner had bailed out Art financially three or four times," said Policy. "I knew the commissioner [Paul Tagliabue] had once done some work for Al when Paul was a young lawyer. I knew how important ownership was to the success of a franchise, and with Al behind us, we'd never have to cut a corner."

It took several weeks and a few meetings, but Policy eventually left the 49ers front office to join with Lerner. They recruited Bernie Kosar to be a spokesman, and also to erase the scarlet letter of having been with Modell. Cleveland mayor Mike White endorsed the group. At the end of August 1998, there was another NFL owners meeting. There were seven bidders for the Browns, and all seven appeared in front of the NFL owners. They still refused to select a group. So what if training camp for the expansion team would start in 10 months? These guys were in no hurry. The Browns weren't their team. They didn't care that they were making it impossible for the Browns to be a contender for a few years by their delays that would rob the new owners of a chance to hire a top-notch front office and coach. In fact, they would never say it publicly, but they wanted the Browns to flounder. They were embarrassed by how Jacksonville and Carolina became contenders in their second seasons. They were doing everything possible to stack the competitive deck against the new Browns.

Modell was vehemently opposed to Lerner. He believed Lerner abandoned him after Lerner began taking some heat for the move. Modell was very upset when it appeared Lerner was distancing himself from the moves he orchestrated to help Modell make the right contacts in the Baltimore power structure. Modell believed Lerner was pointing the entire finger of blame at the new owner of the Baltimore Ravens, and Modell kept telling people, "Wasn't it Al who advised me to move to Baltimore?" Modell wondered why Lerner was suddenly getting a free pass from most of the Cleveland media. Modell also liked the Dolan group, headed by the brothers Charles and Larry Dolan. He introduced them to Bill Cosby, who had an interest in owning a piece of an NFL franchise. Supposedly, the NFL was very excited about the possibility of minority ownership, even a small percentage as would have been the case with Cosby.

Meanwhile, Lerner thought Modell should be grateful for the help he received and the Baltimore deal, and that Modell had no reason to complain about anything. Lerner realized that he was left in Cleveland to take the heat for Modell, who had moved to Baltimore. Maybe both men were right about each other. Certainly, Modell didn't like the idea of Lerner owning the new Browns because his old friend would suddenly be the new hero in Modell's old hometown. Also, Modell had to fear Lerner's bankbook. The new Browns would play in the same division as Baltimore, and Modell hated the idea of losing to Lerner. He lobbied owners against Lerner. He spoke to them as a group, and to individuals informally. Lerner had to consider this an act of betrayal. After all, Lerner did help Modell stay alive financially in Cleveland, and then Lerner helped facilitate the move to Baltimore so Modell could keep the team. And this was how Modell paid him back?

On September 7, 1998, the NFL had yet another meeting, this time in Chicago. The final two bidders were Lerner and the Dolan family. Lerner bid $530 million, the Dolans $525 million. Lerner set a record for buying the most expensive pro franchise in the history of American sports. The previous high was $350 million paid by Rupert Murdoch's Fox Group for the Los Angeles Dodgers baseball team. That was on March 19, 1998.

Several teams have since sold for more than the Browns, but the NFL found a way to run up the price to a record level. Excluding Modell, the other owners each received $18 million of the Browns' expansion fee. After opposing Lerner for months and even early in what became the final meeting, Modell finally voted for Lerner. The first four votes were 21 for Lerner, seven for the Dolans, two abstaining. NFL rules required 23 of the 30 teams to vote for the same bidder. After Modell finally saw that Lerner would eventually prevail, Modell gave a brief speech in favor of his old friend, and Lerner was approved 29-0, with Oakland abstaining.

Al Lerner had the Browns, and he also had more problems than he ever imagined.

5. No Time to Lose

Even though Bill Belichick and Art Modell were doing everything in their power to alienate the Browns fans in the '90s, I still remained faithful. I take pride in the fact that I attended the last playoff game ever held at the old stadium (a 20-13 wild card win over the Patriots). When the Browns signed Rison that next season, I, like a lot of people, immediately began to think one thing— Super Bowl. Not ever getting there by then should have smartened me up. Some people I know can't root for the reincarnated Browns like they did the originals. To me, my love for this team never ended. When they came back in 1999, life was suddenly complete again. Sure, the team was terrible, but it didn't matter to me—the Browns were back where they belonged.

—Dan Gilles

Most fans just wanted their Browns back. They were like the father in the New Testament story of the prodigal son. That's where Jesus talks about a young man who can't wait for his father to die so he can receive his inheritance. Instead, he asks his father for his cut right now; in the Jewish culture, that was like telling your father, "I wish you were dead!" The kid takes the money, blows it on parties, women, and wine, and ends up broke in a pigpen. He remembers that his father's servants live better than he does at that moment, so he goes home, prepared to apologize. The father sees the son a long way off, and runs to him. Before the son can even blurt out his offer just to be a servant, the father throws a party, gives him a special robe and ring, and welcomes him home—all is forgiven. The father is ready to start all over again with the wayward son.

For most Browns fans, that's how it was when Al Lerner was awarded the team and 1999. They dropped their anger at the NFL. They decided Lerner was a pretty good owner, after all. They were ready to take whatever they could. Like the father of the prodigal son, they believed some football, even expansion football, was better than no football.

I received several calls from fans saying, "I'd rather have an expansion team than a Browns team owned by Art Modell."

Other fans told me, "If this was the price we had to pay to get rid of Modell, it was worth it!"

Some rationalized, "I'm OK with Al Lerner. At least he got Modell out of here."

I kept reminding them that expansion was painful, and it could take years for the team just to be decent. I mentioned I'd rather have the old Browns with a core of some decent players such as Vinny Testaverde, Rob Brunett, Tony Jones, Anthony Pleasant, Stevon Moore, Keenan McCardell, Tom Tupa, and Derrick Alexander. At least it was something to work with; the new Browns had nothing.

Consider that the NFL gave the expansion Houston Texans 1,068 days between the owner being chosen and the first game in 2002. The expansion Carolina Panthers had 677 days before their first game in 1995, the expansion Jacksonville Jaguars had 642 days before their first game in 1995. The so-called "modern era" of football is generally considered to have started in 1960, with the election of NFL Commissioner Pete Rozelle and the creation of the American Football League. Since that time, the NFL has approved 11 expansion franchises. Only two teams—Dallas (240 days) and New Orleans (320 days)—were given less time to prepare to play than the Browns:

Team	Owner chosen	First NFL game	Prep days
Houston Texans	10/06/1999	09/08/2002	1,068
Carolina Panthers	10/26/1993	09/03/1995	677
Tampa Bay Buccaneers	12/05/1974	09/12/1976	647
Seattle Seahawks	12/05/1974	09/12/1976	647
Jacksonville Jaguars	11/30/1993	09/03/1995	642
Minnesota Vikings	01/28/1960	09/17/1961	598
Cincinnati Bengals	05/24/1967	09/06/1968	471
Atlanta Falcons	06/30/1965	09/11/1966	438
Cleveland Browns	09/08/1998	09/12/1999	369
New Orleans Saints	11/01/1966	09/17/1967	320
Dallas Cowboys	01/28/1960	09/24/1960	240

The Browns are one of only five teams in the modern era to have less than 18 months to begin operations. Every other franchise that began on short notice was originally proposed in the 1960s, when the AFL and NFL were competing for markets. In fact, both Minnesota and Dallas had already received AFL franchises when the NFL awarded teams to both cities. Since the merger, the NFL has clearly believed that a team requires about two years to hire staff and scout players. The shortest preparation period since the merger (642 days, to Jacksonville) was 273 days—a full nine months—longer than the Browns received.

No matter how you felt about the Browns coming back, do you understand what the NFL did to your team? How the league treated you with complete disrespect? The extremely short preparation period was purely the creation (and fault) of the NFL. Modell announced his intention to move the Browns on November 6, 1995—1,376 days before the new Browns played their first regular-season game.

On February 8, 1996, Tagliabue said the NFL would guarantee Cleveland a team beginning in 1999—either a relocated franchise or an expansion team, at the league's discretion.

Bottom line?

The NFL spent 911 days deciding who should be the next Browns owners. That's an outrage, and it had dramatic implications for the team and fans.

Carmen Policy knew trouble loomed.

"In March of 1998, [Steelers owner] Dan Rooney and I both told the Commissioner that they had to commit to an ownership group in Cleveland—NOW!" he said. "I was still with the 49ers. They kept talking about playing in 1999, and they weren't even close to picking an owner in the spring and early summer of 1998."

Policy later joined Al Lerner and after they were awarded the franchise on September 8, 1998, he had to hire everyone—on both the football and business sides of the operation. The NFL had put former NFL executive Joe Mack in charge of collecting scouting reports and Mack hired a few scouts, but Mack was not going to run the team. The NFL continued to stall and try to drive up the price while leaving the Cleveland market open as leverage for other teams to use as a threat to move—to get new stadiums and better leases.

As for the fans?

The NFL assumed you'd be there, no matter what: Buying tickets. Buying jerseys, jackets, and caps. Buying just about anything orange and brown. Even buying PSLs for the right to buy season tickets! Policy believed he could put the business side of the operation in order in time for a 1999 kickoff. But he was very worried about the football end, and that's what mattered most. Marketing and service people can make the stadium a good experience for fans, but the bottom line is winning. Yes, the NFL gave the Browns extra draft picks between each of the seven rounds, but if the scouts and player personnel people don't have time to do the proper research . . . well, you end up with what the Browns did for several years.

Had Lerner been granted the franchise in the spring of 1998, Policy could have hired a coach and general manager before the 1998 season, then have them spend that year scouting the college players and pros who would become available in the expansion draft.

"That's what we had in Houston," said Chris Palmer, the first coach of the new Browns and now offensive coordinator with the Houston Texans. "It's a night-and-day difference. I spent a year scouting after leaving Cleveland and our first regular-season game in Houston. We had so much more time to prepare. I wish we could have had this in Cleveland."

Instead, the Browns had to wait until the end of the 1998 season—basically, January 1999—to begin interviewing coaches and general manager candidates. And the expansion draft was February 9, 1999.

In December of 1998, Policy said he told Lerner, "Al, we have to ask the NFL to give us another year to get ready."

"We can't," said Lerner. "The city was promised a team in 1999. The stadium is nearly completed. Tickets have been sold. The TV networks are committed to a schedule. We're playing in the Hall of Fame game in August. It's too late."

Policy was telling me all this in the spring of 2004.

"None of us knew what we were facing," Policy said. "I thought I did, but I didn't. Not even after all I'd been through in 20 years in the NFL. The fans were in love with the Browns being back on the field, not really understanding the concept of an expansion team. But an expansion team is an expansion team."

Comparing the preparation time to the winning percentage in the first season strongly suggests that there is a correlation between the two. The 1999 Browns—who had the third-shortest period of time to prepare for their first season—also had the third-worst winning percentage in their first season. One of the teams with a poorer record (the 1960 Cowboys) had even less time to prepare. The teams given the most time to prepare (the 1995 Panthers and 2002 Texans) had the two highest first-year winning percentages.

Team	W/L %	Prep time, days
Carolina Panthers	.438	677
Houston Texans	.250	1,068
Jacksonville Jaguars	.250	642
Minnesota Vikings	.214	598
Atlanta Falcons	.214	438
New Orleans Saints	.214	320
Cincinnati Bengals	.214	471
Seattle Seahawks	.143	647
Cleveland Browns	.125	369
Dallas Cowboys	.042	240
Tampa Bay Buccaneers	.000	647

Want to feel even worse?

Only one expansion general manager (Dallas) had less time to prepare for opening day than new Browns GM Dwight Clark.

Why do I still care? Why did I drive seven hours in 1988 to see a preseason game? Why did my mom agree to spend about one-third of her life savings for a satellite antenna in 1988 to watch Browns games when we lived in Georgia? Why did my three daughters' baptisms in '78, '79, and '82 turn into Browns parties? Why did I sit in the car alone in 1966 at a family picnic to listen to a Browns/Packers game on the radio? Why am I already planning my 40th anniversary of attending my first Browns game (October 31, 1965, they lost to the Vikings)? Why did my daughter and I cry when we drove by the remnants of the old stadium when only the concrete from gate C still stood? Why did I hold my daughter and cry after the new Browns finally won a home game and it was against the STEELERS? Why did my daughter and I sit in the stands last December after the Atlanta game in 2002 and wait for the outcome of the Miami/New England game? Well before I became a born-again Christian, it was like a religion. But today I realize why it is a treasured shared experience. I shared it with my mom and today I share it with my daughter. It is a shared experience that bonds the generations.

—Jim Yearsin

6. The Wrong Guy

I'm 45 and I've had season tickets since I moved back to
Ohio in 1986. I bought two seats even before I had a place
to live. I'd take my dad to the Steelers games, my brother
to the Bengals, my brother-in-law to the Oilers. The others
were divided among friends.

It's all because growing up as a kid in Mansfield, I'd go
to games with my dad on a chartered bus. My dad was on
the road a lot and we didn't have as much time as most
kids with their dads, so the Browns games were special.

—Tim Barney

What the new Browns needed was an experienced, successful general manager to take on one of the biggest chal-
lenges in the history of the NFL.

What they got was Dwight Clark.

And Dwight Clark wasn't even supposed to be the new
general manager.

Really.

In the spring of 2004, Carmen Policy told me that Clark
"was put into a position that he was never intended to have."

"He was supposed to coordinate football decisions between the coach and general manager," said Policy.

I was stunned.

Finally, I said, "Sort of a Pete Garcia type?"

Policy agreed.

Garcia is the right-hand man of current Browns coach Butch Davis. He serves as chief scout and advisor. He was the recruiting coordinator for Davis when they were together at Miami University. He makes recommendations, but the final decision rests with Davis. In some interviews, Davis has downplayed Garcia's role in talent evaluation, stressing his organizational skills instead.

"Dwight really wasn't supposed to be responsible for all the personnel decisions," said Policy.

Then who was?

"We had conversations with a few established general managers," he said. "But because of the task at hand, their demands were so high, really excessive—as in wanting a piece of ownership."

The point Policy made was that he and Lerner didn't want to add another owner.

But there was more.

"I also didn't think we could hire someone like [former Browns pro personnel assistant] Scott Pioli," he said.

Why not?

"Because he was associated with the Belichick regime here," he said. "I didn't think it was a good idea to bring in anyone from those days. I didn't think the fans would give the guy a fair shake."

That now sounds bad, especially since Pioli has emerged as one of the NFL's top executives with Belichick in New England. Fans would hold a parade for him down Euclid Avenue if Pioli were to join the Browns today. But in 1999 before Belichick had resurrected his career with New England? Before anyone knew much about Scott Pioli, other than he once worked for Belichick in Cleveland? Would you have bought that man running the new Browns when so many would still blame him as part of the front office that ruined the old Browns?

For what it's worth, I once asked Pioli if he would have been interested in the Browns job back in 1999.

"Absolutely," he said.

Was he ever contacted?

"No," he said. "But I love the city. I love the fans. I love the history of the franchise. It's just a great football town and the fans deserve a team they can be proud of. They've been through so much."

Policy said he felt the pressure of the season coming, and someone had to run the front office. He'd had a long relationship with Clark, dating back to the 49ers in 1983 when Policy was the team's general counsel, Clark a star receiver. In 1989, Policy hired the newly retired Clark to work in the team's marketing department. At that point, Policy had been named the 49ers executive vice president. The coach was George Seifert, who made the key football personnel decisions along with John McVay, whose title was vice president of football operations. Policy was in charge of the business side of the operation. Clark worked his way up in the 49ers front office. He became an administrative assistant (1990), then coordinator of football operations and player personnel. That was from 1990 to '94.

In 1995, Clark was promoted to executive vice president and director of football operations, meaning he had the basic duties of a general manager working with Siefert.

You can always argue about who is responsible for certain draft picks or free agent signings. While Policy and Clark were in charge of the 49ers from 1995 to '98, their drafting record was mixed at best. Policy has never made claims about being a great judge of football talent, so the strongest voice about picking players belongs to Clark. Too often, he called out the wrong names:

- In 1995, he traded two No. 1 picks to the Browns to se-lect J. J. Stokes, who was mostly an average pro receiver. He also gave up a second-round pick as compensation for signing free agent defensive back Marquez Pope, another average player who later resurfaced with the new Browns.
- In 1996, the 49ers had their best pick of the Clark era, receiver Terrell Owens in the third round. But none of the other picks ended up with significant NFL careers.
- In 1997, they had only three draft picks: quarterback Jim Druckenmiller, Marc Edwards, and Greg Clark. Those were their choices in the first three rounds. Drucken-miller played only eight NFL games. Edwards was a journeyman fullback who later played with the new Browns. Clark had a short and unmemorable career as a receiver.
- In 1998, Clark had his last draft with the 49ers, and by far his best. R. W. McQuarters became a starting NFL cornerback. Jeremy Newberry (second round) and Lance Schulters (fourth round) made Pro Bowl teams. Sixth-rounder Fred Beasley became a useful blocking fullback who made the Pro Bowl in 2003.
- Clark and Policy were very aggressive in signing free agents—some good, some not. But the 49ers were also fined $600,000 by the NFL for violating salary cap rules. The franchise was usually in salary cap trouble, some years $25 million over, which led to cuts in the follow-ing season that caused problems. Policy and Clark are not viewed favorably by many 49er fans for their final

years together, and the new 49ers front office blamed their spending habits for putting them in salary cap purgatory for several seasons, stopping the team from bidding on free agents and keeping some of their own.

- In Clark's four years running the 49ers, their record was an impressive 48-16. But they ceased to be a factor in the playoffs. In one season, they lost in the NFC championship game. But in the other three, they were booted out in the first round. In the first two years after Clark and Policy left for Cleveland (1999 and 2000), the 49ers were a combined 10-22 as they had to cut veteran players to put their salary cap in order.

I look at that list and still ask, "Why Dwight Clark?"

I ask, "How hard did Policy look for someone else?"

I wonder, "Did Policy simply settle for Clark because it was easy and comfortable, and he knew he could have major input if he wanted it without any real interference?"

"We needed to get things done, and get them done quickly," said Policy. "I knew Dwight was a tireless worker. He never slept in those first few months. No one did. We couldn't wait. We had to move forward."

The new Browns' first media guide came out before the 1999 season, and in Clark's biography, we're told: "He is responsible for all aspects of the Browns' football operations . . . he will oversee all aspects of professional and college personnel, including contract negotiations and salary cap considerations. One of his most important responsibilities will be to work closely and be in direct contact with the head coach on all matters affecting the team."

To the credit of the media guide, it makes no great claims about Clark as head of the 49ers front office, simply saying he was responsible for scouting, player personnel, contract negotiations, salary cap management. The same stuff he did with the Browns.

I remember the first time I met Clark, which was November 30, 1998. He was introduced as vice president in charge of player personnel, which is a long title meaning general manager. It was five weeks after Lerner and Policy took control of the team. It also was only about nine months before the first game. The expansion draft was five weeks away. They still had no coach. Dwight Clark had very little time and probably no chance to make this work, especially given his rather limited experience and spotty record when making the major decisions for the 49ers.

Here is where you can blame the media a bit. Not necessarily for Dwight Clark. Why would anyone in northern Ohio push for the hiring of a 49ers hero who was originally from Kinston, North Carolina, and later played at Clemson? Dwight Clark meant nothing to fans here. But no one in the media made a strong case for hiring an experienced and successful general manager. At least, I plead guilty to ignoring it, and I don't recall anyone else making it a crusade. I think because we all were caught up in the excitement of the team returning and speculation about the possible coaching candidates, we forgot this basic football fact: If you don't have a good GM, you won't have a good coach. That's because a coach is at the mercy of his players. A bad coach can ruin a good team, but a good coach can't save a bad team. The best he can do is make it somewhat competitive, perhaps pull an upset or two, but it will still end up under .500. It's true that some coaches run the entire football operation—but very few of them do it well. Those men also happen to be gifted evaluators of talent, and they tend to have strong assistants who help them. Bill Belichick has Scott Pioli in New England. And yes, Jimmy Johnson did have Butch Davis among others.

The critical choice of the GM was mostly ignored by the media and fans. We tended to think with all the draft picks coming—28 in two years—how could they mess up?

This is Cleveland, this is our town, these are our teams . . . we should have known better.

When I met Dwight Clark, I immediately liked him. Most people do. As one executive told me, "Dwight is one of those good-looking, sincere guys. He has a way of knowing what to say and you find yourself wanting to believe he can do it . . . but he was just over his head in that job. Very few of us could have pulled it off."

I stretched to write something positive on the day he was hired. I talked about how Clark seemed like a nice man, how he was determined to learn from his mistakes with the 49ers, and how he admitted to some poor picks—rather than trying to pass them off on someone else. I gave him high marks for honesty and dedication. But I was strangely silent on the key part of the job: talent evaluation. Most of us didn't think about any of this. The Browns were coming back, and somehow that was supposed to make everything right with the football world.

Fans cling to the Browns like they are the last life preserver in the boat as it's being capsized in the middle of a hurricane. Somehow, the Browns playing each Sunday is enough to help many fans get through the next miserable six days. And of course, there's the draft, free agency, and training camp to divert our attention.

Being around this sports scene, we know bad things happen to our teams.

And they certainly have with the new Browns.

"I didn't make the picks or evaluate the players," said Policy. "But I hired the guy who did. I put the people in place, so that has to stop at my door."

Policy later moved out of the front office to an early retirement, probably setting up his next move to another team. I think of how he loves the spotlight and revels in winning. He hates to be criticized. Losing does eat him up. He generally is a smart guy with a law degree. I just wonder why he put so much of his faith, and of his own football future, in the hands of Dwight Clark. Down deep, he had to know Clark's strengths and weaknesses. He knew Clark better than anyone because they'd worked together for so long. He had to know that Clark was not suited for this job, but he hired him anyway. And in the end, that reflects more harshly on Policy than it does on the first general manager of the new Browns.

7. "Nothing Went According to Plan"

I worshiped Kosar, Newsome, Byner, Slaughter, Matthews, and the rest. After the Browns lost the 1987 AFC Championship game to "The Drive," I wore my Browns sweatshirt to school the next day to show my support. I was in the sixth grade and my teacher thought that was "cute." But to me, I was doing something important for the team. I remember running to the radio after the Browns beat the Jets in double overtime, waiting for the all "Browns Songs" to play so I could tape them. My mother and father taught me football, and I truly believe watching the games brought us together as a family. I love the Browns today because I was raised to. Things have changed with the move, salary caps, and today's athletes, but I still choose to embrace the team and go along for the ride.
—Ken Keller

There had to be a better way to do this.

A better way for the Browns to hire a coach, put together a front office, and build a team. The more I listened to Carmen Policy talk about the early days of the Browns, the more I realized how nothing went according to his plan, partly because he didn't seem to have a clear vision of what the team needed. This was because Policy had no idea what it meant to start an expansion team. He not only grew up in the NFL with the highly successful 49ers, but that franchise was his only frame of reference. He'd never admit it, but he somehow thought he could recreate the 49ers on the shores of Lake Erie. Of course, the expansion Browns and the 49ers had about as much in common as a Yugo and a Lexus. They both had four wheels, and both thought they belonged on the superhighway, but it wasn't hard to guess which would give a much better ride.

It's possible no NFL executive could have done much better than Policy because of the time constraints and restrictions set by the NFL. But I remember talking to former Browns star Mike McCormick, who was a part of another group hoping to buy the new Browns. McCormick had worked in several NFL front offices, and had been a key part of starting the Carolina Panthers. He had the clearest vision of what the Browns were facing. Policy's was clouded by the 49ers, where Bill Walsh had been the Paul Brown of that franchise, putting a system in place that carried the team forward for nearly two decades. It's much easier to be the president of a team already built by Walsh, than a team with no front office, no coach, no players, and no time.

As Policy looks back, he talks about wanting to hire an established coach. He was interested in Steve Mariucci, who had been Policy's coach with the 49ers. His record for two years was 24-7-1, six of the losses to playoff teams. He was at the top of Policy's list, and there are good reasons. Mariucci was a winning coach who liked offense and already had a relationship with Clark and Policy. Given his choice, it seemed Policy wanted to import as many 49ers to Cleveland as possible, even though he now says that's not necessarily the case. But Mariucci had three years left on his contract, and the 49ers were not about to release him from that obligation. Especially not with Policy and Clark in Cleveland, and Policy having left the 49ers after a dispute with the DeBartolo family. Whatever time Policy spent waiting for Mariucci was probably wasted.

Policy focused on Mariucci because he knew him, he trusted him, and because Mariucci was an "offensive-minded coach."

"We planned to take a quarterback with the first pick," Policy explained. "We were not going to the Super Bowl right away, so we wanted a coach who would take care of the major investment [the quarterback to be drafted]."

Policy also had an eye on Mike Holmgren, whose contract as head coach in Green Bay was to expire at the end of the season. But Policy talked about Holmgren during the 1999 season, and Holmgren was still coaching the Packers. At a December 1 luncheon, a fan asked Policy about hiring Holmgren. Policy began his answer by saying he couldn't discuss the subject "because it would be tampering."

He should have stopped right there.

What happened next illustrates a weakness for Policy. He loves to talk. He handles the language well. But here's something to remember: The more you say, the more likely you are to say something wrong.

And Policy said more.

"Let's just say if there's a head coach out there who has won a Super Bowl, who has been to another Super Bowl, who is coaching a team in contention this year, who is an offensive-minded coach, looking to perhaps move when the season is over . . . "

Only one man fit that description.

Two days later, the NFL fined Policy $10,000 for what he said at the luncheon.

It seemed Policy thought he could send Holmgren a message through the media that the Browns job could be his, and lure him by waving Al Lerner's fat bankbook like a red cape in front of a bull . . .

Or else, Policy knew he had no chance at Holmgren, but simply wanted to impress the fans by letting them know he planned to pursue a big-name coach. Either way, it was a rather amateurish mistake from an experienced executive who should have known better. Besides, Holmgren was not about to come to Cleveland. He wanted to run his own show, be GM/coach. Two days before Policy's luncheon remarks, Clark had been hired as the Browns GM. Holmgren eventually moved to Seattle, where his deal gave him total control of the football operations.

Something never reported is that Policy also considered respected Tennessee coach Jeff Fisher.

"They wouldn't let us talk to him. Instead, he got a contract extension," said Policy.

Policy was handicapped because he couldn't speak to any coaches until the end of their regular seasons. He also couldn't contact head coaches under contract, unless their teams would allow it—which they were not about to do.

There was yet another restriction, this one self-imposed.

"As I mentioned, I didn't think it was wise to bring in anyone from the old [Belichick-Modell] regime," he said. "While I liked Nick Saban, I didn't even interview him."

Saban had been Belichick's defensive coordinator, and later a respected college coach. In 1998, he was head coach at Michigan State. Was it correct to paint a scarlet letter next to Saban's name, turning him into a leper because of his association with Belichick? Debatable. But at that point, I doubt Saban would have been a serious candidate under any circumstances. He was a defensive coach who had not been a head coach in the NFL. Also, Saban had to know the Browns job was a career suicide mission and he would have been wise to not bother to pursue it. Especially since he would be courted by other colleges such as LSU, where he was hired after the 1999 season.

Policy ended up taking the well-traveled road taken by most NFL executives—the one that leads to the "hot" assistants. These generally are offensive coordinators from Super Bowl teams, or at least teams that went deep into the playoffs.

The thinking is this: "OK, we can't get that team's head coach, but maybe we can get his assistant. And maybe that guy had something to do with that team's winning. And maybe some of it will rub off on us."

But the executive has no clue if any of that is true!

Head coaches will tell you how important it is to have great coordinators, and how those coordinators are crucial to the team's success.

No doubt, that is true.

But the head coach is still the head coach.

The coordinator is not a head coach, regardless of his title. Some of these guys are called associate head coaches or have other impressive labels next to their names for a variety of reasons ranging from ego to a bigger paycheck to convincing ownership to increase this guy's salary because he has this new title.

But the head coach is still in charge.

The coordinator . . . the associate head coach . . . the Almost Grand Pooh-bah . . . is still an assistant coach. That means he does what the head coach says.

The Browns' coaching search certainly wasn't Carmen Policy's finest moment as he prowled the aisle of NFL coordinators. Often, that is as reliable as buying a lottery ticket to pay the mortgage. No one is really sure what an assistant will do as a head coach unless he has been a head coach before. Just to prove the point, when Baltimore hired Brian Billick, the former Minnesota coordinator was supposed to be an offensive genius, a great developer of quarterbacks. And he led the Ravens to the Super Bowl, right? But how did he do it? Defense, defense, and more defense. He changes quarterbacks more times than Art Modell changed his story about why he moved the Browns. Billick has been with the Ravens since 1999 and he has yet to have a quarterback whom he really seems to trust. But his defense will knock your head off, squeeze it, and hand it back to you—talking trash the whole time. The offensive will run the ball down your throat, leaving cleat marks all over your head. The passing game looks like something Woody Hayes always feared, when the former Ohio State coach said, "Three things can happen when you throw a pass, and two of them are bad."

The Ravens were right when they introduced Billick as "a winner." But he certainly didn't do it how they expected. This is not a knock on Billick, who is one of the league's better coaches. It just shows how little teams really know when they hire these assistants.

Just because a coordinator plays a certain style doesn't mean he'll do it when he's the head coach. Because the coordinator is following the general direction of his head coach. Nor do recommendations mean much. Most head coaches will wildly praise their coordinators when they are considered for a job elsewhere, or why else did they promote the guy to coordinator in the first place? Hiring a lousy coordinator is a poor reflection on a head coach. Sometimes, a head coach may endorse his coordinator for another job because the head coach really doesn't mind if the man leaves. Maybe they clashed. Maybe the head coach wants to hire someone else. Maybe it's just like business, where a candidate has excellent references from his old job because they can't wait to get the guy out the door!

Occasionally, the head coach tells the unmitigated truth: His coordinator is an excellent man, a good leader and communicator, and knows how to deal with the pressures of the job.

But if you're in Policy's sharp three-piece suit, how do you know the difference?

That was the situation as Policy began sorting through the deck of that season's exalted coordinators. Some of the names were Gary Kubiak (Denver), Chris Palmer (Jacksonville), Sherman Lewis (Green Bay), Andy Reid (Green Bay), Bill Callahan (Oakland), and Billick (Minnesota).

Former 49ers head coach George Seifert was available, but he seemed to have little interest in the Browns. It could have been the front office, or perhaps just the incredible burden of coaching an expansion team. Besides, Carolina offered him a chance to be GM/coach, something not available with the Browns.

"Know what I heard from most coaches?" said Policy. "They told me that they wanted to be my second coach."

That's a common sentiment in pro sports. The initial expansion coach takes the bullet. His body is thrown under the train, leaving track marks on his psyche and losses on his record. He's lucky to survive three years and never is truly appreciated for the thankless job he did.

Policy did bring in a former head coach, Art Shell, who had a winning record in Oakland. But he was considered by most NFL executives best suited to be an assistant, and his offense in Oakland was not exactly the second coming of the Kardiac Kids. They'd never admit it, but interviewing Shell gave the Browns the ability to say they talked to a minority about the job.

Policy's man was Billick, whom he interviewed for seven hours. Policy raved to the media about Billick after their session was over, adding, "Brian Billick will be a head coach in the 1999 season."

Policy was right.

Policy wanted it to be in Cleveland.

Policy may have blown that chance.

We'll never really know. But this much is certain: While Policy was talking to other assistant coaches, he was waiting for Billick's season to end in Minnesota. When the Vikings lost in the 1999 NFC Championship game to Atlanta, the Browns dispatched Dwight Clark on a private jet to Minnesota to get Billick and bring him back to Cleveland. The Browns had called Billick's agent to inform him of the plan. The agent contacted Billick, who said he had no intention of talking to the Browns or anyone else for a few days. He was emotionally drained. Clark arrived only a few hours after the Vikings' disappointing defeat, still intent on whisking Billick back to Cleveland. Billick told Clark he was upset by the loss and didn't want to make any decision that night, or even the day after the game. He also mentioned he had an interview in Baltimore later that week, which was common knowledge. The Browns pushed Billick to come to Cleveland, as they wanted to sign him before Modell could. Meanwhile, the Ravens' David Modell called Billick to say, "I know that game was rough on you. Just take your time. We'll talk whenever you feel ready."

Billick appreciated that approach so much more than the

pressure he was receiving from the Browns. Policy was offended that Billick wanted to wait and talk to Baltimore. He decided that if Billick wasn't totally sold on the Browns, then he no longer was buying Billick. He released a statement that they had "significant philosophical differences related to the opportunities in an expansion situation. It is our desire to move forward with our coaching search without Brian Billick being part of that consideration."

Would Billick have taken the Baltimore job anyway, even if the Browns were patient?

We'll never know.

But this much is certain: By trying a power play, they shoved Billick into the lap of Ravens General Manager Ozzie Newsome. They did this despite not having a clear No. 2 guy waiting. They seemed to do this as much out of anger as any real plan. Billick was the same guy loved by Policy in the first interview. The only "philosophical differences" had to do with Billick not wanting to play the game the Browns' way.

"I just don't think Brian wanted the challenge of an expansion situation," Policy said in the spring of 2004.

Finally, Policy turned to Chris Palmer, who had been a respected offensive coordinator in Jacksonville. He was hired four days after the Billick blowup. And in the end, Billick should be very grateful.

8. Hired and Doomed

I still follow and love this team because it's what we DO. I'm a son, a brother, a father, and a Browns fan. They're all connected. When the Browns win, we win. When the Browns lose, we lose. We've lost quite a bit in the last nine years! But when it happens, we'll have been there for it from Red Right 88, the Drive, the Fumble, the Move, and everything that has happened since they came back.

—Tim Retchless

The Browns could have hired Andy Reid as their new head coach, and Reid went on to become a major success in Philadelphia.

But it wouldn't have mattered.

In fact, the Browns didn't even interview Reid.

Not that it mattered.

They could have hired Marvin Lewis, who has helped turn around Cincinnati.

Not that it mattered.

John Fox was available, and he coached Carolina to the 2003 Super Bowl.

That's right, it didn't matter, either.

At this point, the Browns were such a disaster that Paul Brown could have come back from the grave and it still wouldn't have mattered. OK, Paul Brown may have been the one guy who could have saved this situation, but only if they gave him a five-year contract and stayed out of his way for all five years.

But in the reality of the 1999 Browns, the new coach was doomed. I knew that the moment I walked into Chris Palmer's office on January 22, 1999. It was the day after he had been hired, less than eight months before the first game. Palmer sat at a huge table, packed with media guides.

"What are you doing?" I asked.

"Looking for assistants," he said.

I stared at the media guides.

"The NFL won't let us hire anyone who is under contract," he explained. "So I'm putting together a list of guys who have been fired. In between, I'm making some calls and taking some calls."

I started to ask why he didn't have someone else do it, and then I realized—there was no one else!

He had no staff.

"I don't even have a secretary," he said.

"It's bad news," I said.

"It's expansion," he said.

Suddenly, I knew why Baltimore looked very good to Brian Billick, even with Modell.

Looking back, the Browns' method of picking a coach was rushed and panicky. Once Policy couldn't get an established coach, he showed little creativity—and too much desperation. He wanted someone to coach his beloved West Coast offense, which features a lot of short passes with an occasional downfield throw to keep the defense honest. Or maybe he wanted someone with a "wide open offensive philosophy," as he told some friends. Palmer was not a West Coast offense guy. He preferred to "stretch the field," to use the vertical passing game and try for big plays—at least, that was his theory.

But it didn't matter.

He had no assistant coaches, no players, no strong direction from the front office—and in the end, no hope.

Policy's decision not to talk to defensive coaches meant he passed on Tampa Bay's Herman Edwards, the Giants' John Fox, and Pittsburgh's Jim Haslett. All became head coaches. Reid was Green Bay's quarterback coach, but they skipped him because they thought he could use more experience. He wasn't a coordinator. That didn't stop Philadelphia from taking Reid, who was one of the voices in the draft room urging the Eagles to draft Donovan McNabb with second pick in 1999, right behind Tim Couch.

Now, suppose the Browns had picked McNabb over Couch . . .

That would have mattered.

But would Reid have taken Couch over McNabb?

No one knows for sure. We just know the Eagles needed a quarterback and had McNabb ranked over the Browns' other 1999 draft possibility, the overrated Akili Smith. Reid did say that McNabb reminded him of Brett Favre; remember, Reid was Favre's quarterback coach in Green Bay.

Or how about this? Suppose Chris Palmer had been hired in Philadelphia, and Reid with the Browns? Who would still be the head coach of those teams today? Palmer would be a safer bet.

Whoever was on the Browns sideline, he was doomed for failure—even if the coaching search had not been flawed.

"I knew it was going to be difficult," Palmer told me in the spring of 2004. "I didn't know it would be a mess. My first day on the job, they were still building the offices. There were no people. We were less than nine months from our first game."

Then he thought about Billick passing up the Browns for Baltimore.

"I was wondering if there was something about the Cleveland situation that I didn't see," he said. "Brian knew the people with the Browns more than I did because he had been in San Francisco with Carmen for a while. I'm sure Carmen told Brian that they planned to be patient, just like he told me. I knew Brian was their guy, and he turned them down. Maybe he knew they weren't going to be patient."

Maybe that, and maybe more.

Policy kept telling everyone, "We hired a very good guy in Chris Palmer."

That was true. It also was an attempt to contrast Palmer with the moody Belichick.

Baltimore also interviewed Palmer, and he probably would have been the Ravens' choice had they not won the battle for Billick. So maybe the Browns didn't do such a bad job finding a coach—they just threw their new coach into a really bad job.

Meanwhile, Browns fans did not understand expansion, because Cleveland has not been an expansion town. The Indians have been around forever. The Cavaliers started in 1970, but the NBA usually isn't on the radar screen of the average northeast Ohio sports fan—unless the Cavaliers are playing extremely well or have LeBron James. Few fans remember the dismal early seasons under Bill Fitch, when John Warren made a wrong-way basket and it took them SIX years to finally have a winning record and make the playoffs.

The Browns sort of were an expansion team when they joined the All-American Football Conference in 1946, but it was a brand-new pro league to rival the established NFL. The Cleveland Rams were part of the NFL, but they moved to Los Angeles after the 1945 season. The Cleveland Rams drew only 73,000 fans over four games, and 32,178 for the 1945 NFL

Championship game. At this point, Cleveland was not a pro football town.

But a man named Mickey McBride thought otherwise, as he bought a franchise in the new pro league and hired Paul Brown as GM/coach. So the new Browns were an expansion team in an expansion league. Everyone was pretty much equal. Give Paul Brown a fair shot to put together a team, and you get a champion.

Why this history lesson?

It's to underline the fact that Browns fans had no real background in expansion. The older fans recalled the Cleveland Rams winning that 1945 NFL title, then moving to L.A. They remembered Paul Brown coming in and having a 12-2 season, winning the 1946 All-American Football Conference title. They talk about players signed by Brown who became stars: Marion Motley, Otto Graham, Mac Speedie, Dante Lavelli, and Lou Groza were all members of those first Cleveland Browns.

This wasn't an expansion team, it was a dynasty.

There was something else about Paul Brown: He was the father of modern pro football.

Ever wonder who was the first coach to have his team watch game films? To carry a playbook? To wear face masks? To put coaches in the press box and talk to the head coach on the field through headphones? To hire scouts extensively for the draft? To give his players intelligence tests and quizzes based on the game plan and playbook for that week? To time players in the 40-yard dash because that was the distance of the average punt? If Brown didn't actually invent these things, he was the first coach to consistently implement them. He was far ahead of the competition, his innovations giving him an enormous advantage. It would be like the first baseball manager to use a pinch hitter or a relief pitcher. Or the first basketball coach to use a zone defense or the pick-and-roll play. Paul Brown was like the first man to rub a couple of sticks together and make a fire; the rest of civilization stood in awe. And much the same happened in the late 1940s and 1950s with Paul Brown and his Browns.

But this was a different age.

You couldn't recruit the top players coming back from World War II, as Brown did for his first team. He wrote Groza and others while they were still in the military, promising them a chance to play football for cash if they got out of the war alive and with their limbs intact. Having coached at Ohio State, Brown also was aware of the top high school and college players, especially in the talent-rich Midwest. He outworked, out-thought, and sometimes out-fought his opposition for players with the force of his personality.

Those opportunities didn't exist for Chris Palmer.

When he joined the Browns, Palmer realized the only man who really seemed to understand the challenge was Al Lerner.

"I had tremendous respect for him and what he stood for," said Palmer. "Whatever he did, he was going to do first class. He was going to give you an opportunity to do it right. He knew this couldn't just happen overnight."

Policy and Clark said they were aware of this, too.

But now, you wonder . . .

What was their sole football experience? The San Francisco 49ers, which Bill Walsh had built into a power. Clark and Policy didn't do it, they just inherited it. Policy often talked about the 49ers. It was obvious that they were his frame of reference, but that really didn't apply to the Cleveland situation. Into this quagmire came Palmer, a plump, balding middle-aged guy with wire-rimmed glasses who looked like someone you'd find behind the counter of your local hardware store (which is his family's business back in Brewster, New York). Palmer also had to know he was destined to fail. But if you're Chris Palmer and you're 49 years old and you never played in the NFL, or even at a major college—you know that you'll probably only get one chance like this. Palmer remains a coaching lifer, now the offensive coordinator with the expansion Houston Texans. He has been an assistant with four different NFL teams. He was an offensive coordinator with the New Jersey Generals of the long-gone United States Football League. He was the offensive line coach for the Montreal Concordes of the Canadian Football League. He was head coach at the University of New Haven and Boston University.

Palmer didn't just pay his dues, he seemed to be charged double. He was never given a free pass, never had anyone insist he was a hot coaching commodity. He was just a solid, decent, dedicated man awaiting his chance. He loved every moment of being the coach of the Browns. He appreciated the team's history; the first book he read after getting the job was Paul Brown's autobiography. He read other Browns books. He talked to former players. He listened to the fans as they talked about the heartbreak of the move.

He may have been from New York, but he acted and thought like one of us.

Which is why I always liked Chris Palmer, and to this day have a hard time objectively judging him. I just know that when I wanted to reach Palmer, I could call him at 6 A.M. and he was at the office. I could call at 11 P.M., and he was at the office. He tried to make the Browns a success with his sheer will and volume of hours.

But as former Cavaliers coach Lenny Wilkens once told me, "After a couple of times, it doesn't matter how many times you watch a game film, you still lost. And the guys who can't play still can't play."

And if that was true of any team, it was the 1999 Browns.

Know who was the first player in the history of the new franchise?

Nope, not Tim Couch.

It was center Jim Pyne.

That's what expansion really is about . . . players like Jim Pyne who are either too young, too old, too hurt, too limited, too something that inspired teams to virtually give them away.

Or as Tim Couch later would say, "It's just a bunch of guys thrown together."

When it came to the expansion draft, the NFL had no mercy. If these owners were a judge, they'd give a lethal injection for a parking ticket, especially if you happened to be associated with the Cleveland Browns in 1999. They wouldn't tell you that. They'd smile and talk about the great Cleveland fans, the colorful Dawg Pound, the leadership of Al Lerner and Carmen Policy. But behind the scenes, they had a plan to make sure there would be no repeat of 1995, when Carolina and Jacksonville came into the NFL . . . and made the playoffs in 1996. Browns fans have been so angry at Modell that they've ignored the real villain—THE NATIONAL FOOTBALL LEAGUE, as some deep-voiced announcer would intone as if he were reading from Scripture whenever the league's TV commercials appear. These fine men who love and appreciate Browns fans so much figured it didn't matter what kind of team would be on the field in Cleveland, because the fans had already sold out the stadium before a single player was

on the roster. So who cares if the team stinks? They were embarrassed by the performance of Jacksonville and Carolina in
1996, because those teams made too many of the other franchises look inept. So they made sure no major free agents
were available by the time the Browns were in business. The
teams were careful to sign their key players to contract exten-
sions before the Browns could make offers. This was not a
conspiracy, but teams learned to act quickly with their veterans after seeing Jacksonville and Carolina swoop in and pick
off some talented players after the last expansion. The NFL
also allowed retiring players such as Packers defensive end
Reggie White to be on the expansion list, so Green Bay would
not have to expose a player who could be of some use to the
Browns.

I was in Palmer's office one day as he looked over the expansion list . . .

"There are nine guys available who were there when Jacksonville and Carolina came into the league four years ago,"
he said.

That meant nine players whose teams tried to give them
away in 1995, only they couldn't. They wanted to do it again,
and these stiffs were four years older!

Pittsburgh exposed a player named Will Wohlford, who
was retiring like White. So that allowed the Steelers to protect an extra player.

In 1995, teams could lose up to three players. In 1999, it
was two. That cut down the available talent pool. Not a single
player available to the Browns in 1999 had ever been to a Pro
Bowl.

OK, I hear some fans screaming—KURT WARNER!

Let's go back to February 9, 1999, when that draft was
held. At this point in Warner's career, he had thrown exactly

11 passes in the NFL, completing four, and had a quarterback rating of 47.2. The St. Louis Rams were so impressed with the refugee from the Arena League and NFL Europe, they saw no reason to protect him. No one in the NFL had a high opinion of Warner, who'd attended Northern Iowa University and was a grocery clerk for a while after college. An injury to Trent Green in the Rams' 1999 training camp led to Warner taking over as the starting QB in St. Louis and becoming the MVP. He also had Marshall Faulk in the backfield, not the Browns' Terry Kirby or Karim Abdul-Jabbar (the mediocre tailback, not the Hall of Fame skyhook specialist). Warner was throwing to Isaac Bruce and Torry Holt, not Darrin Chiaverini and Leslie Shepard.

Know what would have happened had Warner been drafted by the Browns? He'd be lucky to know his own name by now, after the physical beating he would have endured.

OK, Warner was in the draft and the Browns missed him.

But they didn't miss much of anyone else, because there was nothing to miss.

Compare that to 2002, when Houston entered the league and 19 former Pro Bowlers were available. Many were past their prime, but at least there was a time when they could play. When the Browns drafted, the list was mostly guys who never did anything in the NFL . . . and never would.

You could look more closely at the expansion draft but, really, why bother? None of these guys are around today. Other than Warner, not much of worth was available. Jim Pyne was the first pick, a center/guard. Good guy Jim Pyne. He probably set a team record for hospital and charity appearances. Jim Pyne loved kids and loved to give. He loved being a member of the Browns. He loved everything about being paid to play pro football. Jim Pyne got it. But like most pro athletes who really appreciate what they have, Jim Pyne was not a terrific player. He was very average before blowing out his knee early in the 2000 season, and played very little after that. The Browns took 37 guys in the expansion draft, and Pyne or offensive lineman Scott Rehberg may have been the best—which isn't saying much. Of the 37 players picked, only 14 made the opening day roster—and we're not talking about trying to crack the lineup of the 1964 Browns here. By 2004, none of the expansion players were left. At the start of the 2004 season, all were gone.

So how would you like to have been Chris Palmer?

9. The Pick

I went to my first Browns game in 1957. I was four years old. My uncle took me and he knew a cop by Gate A, and we got to park right outside the stadium. I was surrounded by fans willing to tell me about the team, the history and teaching me when to cheer. . . .

As Jim Brown evolved into a superstar, I evolved into a superfan. I was lucky enough to go to the 1964 Championship game. I didn't have a ticket, but walked in with my uncle after the game began. . . . Later in my life, I faked an emergency to get home from the army to go to a playoff game . . .

While he was young, my son thought I was nuts to scream for the Browns while watching the game in my living room. But he proudly wore his Browns gear to school as he got the bug after he went to Ozzie Newsome's summer football camp. After the Browns left, I swore off the NFL, watching only high school and college games. I didn't even watch the Super Bowl. I had an arm's length attitude toward the new team until Chris Palmer went out of his way to be kind to a friend. I was hooked . . . again.

Why do I stick it out, watching Carmen & Company stumble and fumble? How could I put a price on four hours of undivided time with my son? I know that our seats will one day be occupied by him and his son, it's a bond my uncle passed to me and I passed to my son . . .

—Henry Dasinger

Confession time: I wrote, said, or even thought little about the Browns taking Donovan McNabb with their first pick in the 1999 college draft. Maybe some fans said it at the time. OK, perhaps a few of them actually believed McNabb was the right guy for the Browns.

But not many.

Not once did the Browns give serious consideration to McNabb, who went on to become a Pro Bowl quarterback in Philadelphia. He hasn't led the Eagles to the Super Bowl, but he is very, very good and has taken the Eagles deep into the playoffs.

Want to know what was really wrong with the Browns in those early years?

They needed a strong general manager. They needed a vision for the team. They needed an NFL-tested front office to figure out how they should play and then get the type of athletes to play that style. For example, Ozzie Newsome built the Ravens into a physically tough, defense-oriented team with a strong running game. Of course he would have liked to put an All-Pro quarterback on the field, but he wanted to win games on the line of scrimmage with sweat, blood, and grunts. Nothing fancy about the Ravens. In St. Louis, Dick Vermeil constructed the Rams to win on artificial turf with a high-scoring team based on speed. Bill Walsh powered the 49ers dynasty with the West Coast offense, which was based on a lot of quick, horizontal passes. Other coaches/general managers have decided on a personality for their teams, then found the players to match. Football is the classic team game. Everyone must play together or everything falls apart.

As I write this, the Browns are heading into the 2004 season. What has been the consistent style that the team wanted to play? Can anyone tell me that? Not what the coaches said for a year or so. I mean, over the long haul . . . the Browns were supposed to look like . . . what?

Fast and skilled? Big and tough? Run and block? Throw and hope?

Anybody have a clue?

For years, it seems the Browns wrote everything in pencil, and kept erasing. If they were Noah building the ark, they would have had 14 elephants and one bird. They would have then run off all the elephants and rounded up 17 tigers, which would have eaten the bird. They would have kept moving things around inside the ark and then forgotten to close all the hatches. When the flood came—or for the Browns, when the tidal wave of a 16-game NFL season hit—the ark was destined to sink.

The reason was a lack of leadership.

Carmen Policy's strength is as a businessman and lawyer. He put together a strong front office in a short time in terms of things such as marketing, public relations, and other behind-the-scenes things necessary for any pro franchise. With Al Lerner's money, Policy could hire some experienced people from other teams to run the business end of the franchise. Policy also had more expertise in this area than he did in football.

But it's football decisions that win games and matter most to the fans, and the big ones were left mostly to Dwight Clark. He worked so hard. He cared so much. He deserves an A for attitude. But he lacked the ability to create what the first president George Bush called "the vision thing."

Other than trying to replicate the West Coast offense of Bill Walsh's San Francisco 49ers, the Policy/Clark team was void of ideas. But when it came time to hire a coach, they didn't find a guy who fit that mold. If Chris Palmer could be considered a disciple of anyone, it would be Bill Parcells.

He believed in a quarterback throwing long, "stretching the field."

If the Browns ended up as a crazy-quilt of players sewed together, it's because the same was true of their philosophies. This was not a good way for a new team to enter into its first draft. This should have been when the Browns made a statement about their franchise. This player should have been the face of how the Browns would play the game.

"We knew we were going to take a quarterback," said Policy.

Why?

"Because if you have a chance to get a franchise quarterback, you take it," said Palmer.

Before the draft, the Browns were talking about three players for the top pick: Tim Couch, Ricky Williams, and Akili Smith.

Why not Donovan McNabb?

"One of the knocks on Donovan was that he'd never won a big game at Syracuse," Palmer said in the spring of 2004. "Donovan had played four years at Syracuse, and I thought what you saw was all you were going to get. Tim had played only three years at Kentucky. What impressed me was his ability to beat people with Kentucky that they had not beaten before. I thought that was a characteristic that some of the other guys didn't have. We were looking for a guy who could rise above the situation and try to make the players better around him. There were other players who could do that, but I thought Tim had more upside."

"The coaches were concerned that McNabb was not the kind of quarterback they needed for their seven-step drop, vertical passing game," said Policy.

The Browns did not work out and interview McNabb with the same intensity that they did Couch and Smith.

"Our coaches formed an opinion based on what they heard from people they knew," said Policy. "Couch was not shoved down anyone's throat. One or two of our scouts liked Ricky Williams, but we knew we had a chance to get a quarterback, and we should take it."

The only notable voice in the Cleveland media pushing for McNabb was *Akron Beacon Journal* football writer Pat McManamon: "Early on, the Browns liked Couch. Two weeks ago, they liked Smith. Today, it's Couch. Me, I've always liked McNabb because of his versatility."

McNabb was the best pure athlete among the quarterbacks, known almost as much for his running ability as his passing at Syracuse. No one ever accused Couch of being a super scrambler. Maybe that is yet another reason why the Browns should have looked harder at McNabb; they'd need a guy who could run away from the pass rush that would be the result of an expansion team with a lousy offensive line.

But for context, when the Eagles drafted McNabb with the No. 2 pick . . . their fans booed.

They wanted Ricky Williams.

So did I.

That was the result of some extensive in-depth scouting on my part—I watched a couple of New Year's Day Bowl games. Ricky Williams was playing for Texas in the Cotton Bowl, and he ran all over Mississippi. Williams carried the ball 30 times for 203 yards and two TDs. He was a bull of a back, his legs like pistons, pumping up and down and shedding the hands and arms of tackles. That was pretty close to a normal game for Williams, who won the Heisman Trophy and set 20 NCAA rushing records at Texas. He looked like a great back, just as he did in other games where I watched him. Even with a bad expansion line, I was convinced Williams would be a productive runner.

Next was Couch in the Outback Bowl. He used the no-huddle offense, and quickly put his Kentucky team in front, 14-3, in the first quarter.

Then there were problems.

Sometimes, Penn State dropped defenders into Couch's favorite passing lanes. Other times, Coach Joe Paterno blitzed his linebackers. Couch ended up being sacked five times. He heaved a couple of hurried interceptions. Often, he would be in a 3rd-and-8 situation, and he'd settle for a four-yard pass. I was underwhelmed, far more impressed with Courtney Brown, the Penn State defensive end who had seven tackles, including a pair of sacks on Couch. That game revealed far more about Couch than I thought at the time. I wrote off many of my concerns to Penn State being a far superior team to Kentucky. But it also showed that Couch was not the kind of quarterback to carry a team and help them overachieve. Few quarterbacks can do that, but the Browns hoped that Couch would be one of the chosen few when they made him the top pick in the draft. They also paid him like it. Fans came to expect it because of the college hype, the exalted draft status, and the need to attach the future star label to someone in a Browns helmet.

Consider that the April 4, 1999, edition of *USA Today* wrote: "That ultra-competitiveness, combined with an almost Brett Favre-like playmaking ability has for months left many NFL personnel men saying Couch is as good as the gaudy numbers he put up in Coach Hal Mumme's Brigham Young-style offense at Kentucky."

USA Today's Richard Weiner wrote: "Couch, as Denver coach Mike Shanahan puts it, seems to the 'safe choice' for the Browns, similar to what Peyton Manning represented for Indianapolis a year ago."

The Browns worked out Couch twice. The first time, they

were uncertain of his arm strength. They also began to flirt with Akili Smith, a gifted athlete with a laser arm who had only one good year at the University of Oregon. After that initial trial, the Browns ranked Smith even with—or perhaps ahead of—Couch. It depends upon who is telling the story. Then, a second workout was a major upgrade, and Dwight Clark was impressed when he caught a pass from Couch that nearly knocked a hole through his chest.

The former star receiver for the 49ers, Clark would later tell reporters, "Tim Couch has always been the guy. He's always been the leader, the one who rallies the troops. He was the best basketball player on his team. He set records in high school. He set records in college. We expect him to set records here."

So remember that back in the spring of 1999, this is what the fans were hearing and reading. Consider the names just mentioned: Peyton Manning and Brett Favre. I reviewed what I wrote before the draft, and I wasn't sold on Couch. In fact, the only consistency about my feelings for Couch is their inconsistency, how they continued to change, how I wanted to believe in him and looked for every excuse to do so—but then would lose faith quickly.

I didn't want to admit the obvious: I never saw stardom in Couch.

Before the draft, I was still leaning toward Williams. I wrote the following:

> Do you take the quarterback who picked up a wobbling Kentucky team and carried it to wins over the likes of Alabama and LSU?
>
> Or do you take the superback who ran over everyone, including Nebraska?

Do you take the quarterback who was humbled by the Penn State defense, seemingly confused by a three-man rush and eight defenders dropping back to cover his receivers? Do you say, "That was just one game, and it sure didn't seem the coaching staff helped Couch adjust."

Or do you say that didn't Penn State give a peek into the future of Vinny Testaverde in a bowl game about a thousand years ago? Like Couch, Testaverde seemed to have the size, strength and arm you'd want from an NFL quarterback—only it took him 12 years to figure out how to play the position.

Is Couch another Testaverde or Ryan Leaf, or is he another Troy Aikman? Are the whispers of a few scouts about his lack of a big time arm to throw long enough to cause doubt, or is it simply the result of his playing in a passing offense that called for him to make short-to-medium throws?

The Browns never seriously considered Williams as their top choice. In retrospect, they would have been better off picking Williams and trading him to New Orleans for the Saints' entire draft in 1999 and two picks in 2000, which is what Washington did. But given the Browns' dismal drafting record in those first few seasons, maybe it would not have made that much difference. The sheer volume of picks—the Browns had 14 of their own plus another eight, making 22 choices—should have produced some quality within the quantity.

But the Browns were determined to pick a quarterback.

"You normally take a quarterback higher than you do other players, because if you don't get a quarterback early, you're not going to get him," said Palmer in the spring of 2004. "You may have a defensive player or someone else on offense rated higher as one player compared to another when considering all positions, but where are you going to get a quarterback? The first three picks that year were all quarterbacks: Couch, McNabb, and Smith. I remember a scout telling me, 'There are 250 million people in the U.S. and you'd think you could find 32 guys who can play quarterback in the NFL.' In my mind, quarterback is the most difficult position to play in all of sports."

Policy said the Browns came close to trading the No. 1 pick. The draft was on a Saturday afternoon. Owner Al Lerner was determined to have the top pick signed before the draft to avoid a holdout. The Browns were talking with Couch and Smith, although Policy said they really had no intention of picking Smith.

"By Friday afternoon, I didn't know if we could make a deal with Couch," said Policy. "We also knew we weren't going to make Smith, Williams, or McNabb the No. 1 pick. We started to look at some trade possibilities, then that night we got a deal done with Couch."

The Browns gave him a $12.25 million bonus, a seven-year deal worth $48 million. It also could be reworked after three years—the Browns giving Couch another $8.75 million in bonus money, which they did after the 2001 season. It was a decision made by Butch Davis.

Problem was, the Browns never gave Couch much help . . . and Couch never could play up to the price they paid for him.

10. Irrational Exuberance

The Browns first game back was magical. We had waited
so long, there was so much promise in the air. It was
the Hall of Fame game in Canton, where it all began for
Ohio football fans. We had Al Lerner and Carmen Policy,
both with Ohio roots. We had a front office that had been
to Super Bowls. We had a good mix of vets and rookies.
We had a No. 1 pick at QB with a great attitude and
background. I played every card I could to get tickets.
There was a B-1 bomber flyover . . . finally, there was
Couch leading a comeback to beat the Dallas Cowboys. I
had chills. . . . It ended a month later on a Sunday night
against the Steelers, but it was still good to have them
back.

—Kyle St. Peter

Browns fans didn't get it.

The NFL threw their new team into a deep pit with no lad-
der, no rope, no hope.

Just a bunch of no-name guys in orange helmets. These
guys weren't real Cleveland Browns. They were just wearing
the uniforms, passing through town, taking up space until
somehow, some way, a real Browns team could eventually
be built.

That was what I was trying to tell the fans, why I wrote
they'd be lucky to win four games.

You'd have thought that I'd just set fire to the American flag!

Four games?

Fans roared back: They'll win more than four games. They have to win more than four games. We're Browns fans. We were just shafted by the NFL and Modell. They owe us more than four games. Maybe not a .500 team, but close. Then the playoffs in 2000.

"Expectations were totally out of control," said Chris Palmer.

The new coach tried to talk about the "process" of building a new team. He almost begged people to be patient. But some of the veteran players heard that and went to Palmer, saying they expected to win now, and so should he, so let's talk playoffs. This story hit the papers, and the fans loved it. Palmer appreciated the players' attitude, but knew they were fooling themselves and bound to look foolish once the team began playing for real.

This was a bad team, period.

Carmen Policy and Dwight Clark had to know that. But even they seemed caught up in the excitement. They talked about not wanting to put limits on what the team could accomplish. They talked about some experienced players that they'd signed, especially on the offensive line. They talked about Ty Detmer, who was supposed to be the quarterback for the first season as Tim Couch was given time to adjust to the NFL. They talked so much, they started to talk themselves into believing it.

No way, no how, no chance of this being anything but a terrible team.

There's not a lot to say about the players on that first team. They were what most fans should have expected from an expansion team. Most Browns fans can't name more than a dozen of them right now. When the 2004 season opened, only cornerback Daylon McCutcheon and kicker Phil Dawson remained from 1999.

Consider that Palmer's coaching staff consisted of men from seven different NFL teams, six different colleges, and one coach whose last stop was the arena football league. When Palmer took the job, there was not a single barbell in what was supposed to be the weight room. These guys barely knew each other's names, and were still trying to find all the important offices and places in the building. Palmer didn't have a working relationship with most of them, and they didn't know how Palmer wanted things done. It was not a comfortable situation for anyone. It also was a product of the NFL's limitations that prevented Palmer and the Browns from hiring assistants who were already under contract with other teams—even if that coach had the desire to move to Cleveland.

As for the players, they were primarily rejects and rookies. The free agents were mostly too old and/or overrated. When Clark and Policy weren't sure what to do, they signed guys who used to play for the 49ers. At one point in that first season, the Browns had at least a dozen players with San Francisco ties. Of that group, only Terry Kirby was a major contributor.

What Palmer needed in the front office was an executive who was a master at bargain hunting and finding useful players in the rummage sales conducted whenever NFL teams had cutdown dates. They needed someone such as New England Player Personnel Director Scott Pioli or Baltimore General Manager Ozzie Newsome. They needed someone with experience and a plan for building a team.

Then the Browns won their first exhibition game.

It was played at Canton's Fawcett Stadium in the shadows of the Hall of Fame. Dallas was the opponent, and no one was taking this game very seriously except Browns fans. They hadn't seen those orange helmets for nearly four years, and they wanted to believe that it was Otto Graham leading their team. Or Frank Ryan. Or Brian Sipe. Or Bernie Kosar. It was a beautiful night, August 9, 1999. It had been sunny all day. Fans had been tailgating and talking football for hours before the stadium gates opened, a Hall of Fame Game record crowd of 25,156. I was just as drunk on optimism as the fans, at least I realize that now as I read what I wrote about the Browns' 20-17 overtime victory against Dallas that night.

So much for scouting reports. So much for Tim Couch being the nervous kid, the 22-year-old who barely needs to shave and doesn't know how to read a playbook. And so much for Ty Detmer, the savvy veteran who has been with four teams in eight years and can quickly grasp any offense.

By halftime, it was official: The Browns had a quarterback controversy.

This is nothing short of astonishing. You can count on one hand the number of practices that Couch had in which he performed like he did yesterday. Maybe one finger. Why mess around, just go ahead and say it: The Kid looked great. OK, it's one preseason game and the Cowboys had their second string defense out there. Couch didn't see any complicated blitzes—blah, blah, blah. But why spoil the fun? Tim Couch came. He played. He conquered. At least on this crisp fall-like Monday night at Fawcett Stadium, Couch was the story, the star, the present and the future . . .

What Tim Couch did was miss on his first pass, then

complete his next NINE. He threw long. He threw short. And best of all, he threw the ball to the guys in the white jerseys. He even scrambled away from the rush and rambled for 8 yards.

Tim Couch played this game as if it were just another night in the NFL for a man who figures he's destined to have his name in the building next to Fawcett Stadium—and we're not talking about the McDonalds.

So maybe I went a little overboard . . .

"The day after that game, we got countless calls from fans wanting to know how to get playoff tickets," recalled former Browns public relations executive director Todd Stewart. "I had worked with the Colts before coming here. Carmen and Dwight had been in San Francisco. Chris had been with several teams. None of us had ever seen anything like it—it was like we were going to the Super Bowl after one exhibition game."

Palmer remembers a certain high-ranking member of the team front office who postponed the family vacation to Europe because he thought the Browns would be in the playoffs. Then came the regular season, a Sunday-night game against Pittsburgh broadcast nationally by ESPN.

We were in the Muny Lot by 8:30 a.m. and psyched to sit in our seats in the Dawg Pound. I took personal gratification in knowing that myself and thousands of others were responsible for the return of the Browns. When the jets flew over and Drew Carey had his say . . . it made me feel vindicated for all the years of love and loyalty for the Browns. The fact that the new stadium brought a new breed of fan . . . and I actually heard people on talk radio

saying Terry Kirby could run for 100 yards . . . none of that
mattered because this was a day for the true fan.

—Russ Hanson

I remember seeing thousands of fans like Russ Hanson as
I walked to the stadium that day. They so wanted to believe
the NFL was doing them a favor, that the league had heard
their demands, felt their pain, and responded. I knew better. I had been to all the league meetings. I knew that these
owners were heartless. I realized that they allowed Modell
to steal the Browns, and then jacked up the price of the new
franchise to $530 million. That was far more than anyone
would have paid for an expansion team in Baltimore. Both
cities got new stadiums, but Browns fans ended up with a far
worse team. I doubt anyone in the stadium realized just how
bad it was . . . and what was to come.

We had done it! Cleveland once again rose from adversity
to celebrate the evening. I was there! It was electric. I
never was so proud to be from Cleveland. The opening show
with Drew Carey, the video, the crowd noise . . . I never
cheered so loud. Then the kickoff . . . The Browns stopped
them . . . and then seeing the Steelers laughing at us all
the way from section 536, row 23, seat 21 . . . the final
score, 43-0 . . . the reality of the season ahead . . . Then
walking to the car thinking this is my team and they are
back, and I love my Browns—43-0 or winning it all, and no
one can take that away from me.

—Matt Edwards

It's because of fans like Matt Edwards that I am writing this
book. They are like Matt Glassman, who five years later still

remembers the Browns stopping the Steelers on a 4th-and-1 situation and, as he wrote, "THE WHOLE PLACE BLEW UP." He added, "There wasn't much to cheer about after that . . . and if I remember right, on his first possession, Couch dropped back to throw, was hit and fumbled."

I don't think most fans are idiots. It's like the birth of a child. For a while, the parents are convinced the child can do anything. Play the cello? Play middle linebacker? Write the great American novel? Be president? Why not have it all? Why put limits on an infant?

> We should have known it was coming . . . we didn't have much talent or time to build a winning organization . . . but we bought into the hype. Why? We were so starved for football to return, we wanted to believe. We always believe.
> —Jeff Williamson

The day after the game, the Browns training complex was a morgue. Policy, Clark, and the rest were shocked by what the Steelers had done to their team. The Browns had managed a grand total of nine yards rushing and two first downs. It seemed the Steelers could have scored 100 points. The Browns defense was on the field for an eternity as the Steelers offense had the ball for 48 of the 60 minutes. The defense was helpless, the offense was even worse. Ty Detmer started at quarterback, seeming rattled and insecure. Couch played near the end of the game, fumbling on his first regular season play. He was 0-for-3 passing, sacked once for seven yards.

"Everyone in the [Browns] building was so caught up in the excitement and the early success of Jacksonville and Carolina, they really lost sight of what was coming," recalled former PR director Todd Stewart. "People were excited about the players just because they were wearing Browns uniforms. In the locker room, guys like Corey Fuller were saying we should make the playoffs. Guys who had been around and should have known . . . I guess they believed it . . . only Chris Palmer seemed to understand what was coming."

Palmer watched the films of that game and saw what he already knew in his heart: This team was going nowhere. Most of the veterans were not going to be around when the team would contend for the playoffs. Some of the rookies had potential. If this season was truly about building for the future, and if Carmen Policy truly was giving Palmer four to five years to make the playoffs, and everyone was sincere about putting together a team the right way—then why wait?

Play now for the future.

So Palmer went to his press conference the day after the debacle and announced that Couch would replace Detmer as the starting quarterback, and Daylon McCutcheon would take over for veteran Antonio Langham at cornerback. Kevin Johnson was already starting at receiver and Rahim Abdullah would soon be starting at linebacker. All of those players were picked in the first three rounds.

Policy and Clark were not happy about this. They thought Palmer was overreacting to one bad game. They believed he should have consulted with them more. They worried that playing the kids would just make a bad situation even more dreadful.

"Chris did all this on his own, after only one game," Policy said in the spring of 2004. "We didn't want to tell him what to do, but we thought he should have at least talked it over with us. We did have a plan in place."

They still didn't get it.

Palmer was taking the long view, the right view. He didn't

know if Couch could be a star, but he knew Detmer was a backup. He didn't know if McCutcheon could be a viable starter, but he knew Langham was finished. He didn't know much about Abdullah, but Clark loved the guy and picked him in the second round. He didn't know much about the future of any of these players, but he saw enough of the present to know it was a waste of time to keep the kids on the bench.

"Hey, if we could get beat 43-0 with veterans, why even do this?" Palmer told himself. "Let's start building this thing right now."

Policy would later say he thought it was a mistake to play Couch so much, so early.

"What difference does it make if he starts after the eighth game or the tenth game?" he said. "He didn't need to take that kind of beating. Our plan was to start Detmer and carry it through at least 10 games. Chris just changed it. Tim will tell you that it was a good thing to play so early, but I wonder . . ."

Palmer disagreed.

"I look back on that first year and I just should have named Tim the starting quarterback from Day One and stuck with him," Palmer said in the spring of 2004. "We all knew Tim was going to start, so we should have started the process right then. I was talking to John Madden about us [the Houston Texans] starting David Carr from Day One, and he agreed. He said it didn't matter if you play your first game or wait three years to start, every quarterback goes through the same things."

The 1999 Browns had two great moments, and the first one was pure luck. They won 21-16 in New Orleans when Couch heaved a long, high, prayer of a pass in the direction of Kevin Johnson in the end zone of the Louisiana Superdome. Johnson came down with the ball on the final play of the game, a 56-yard TD pass. That made the Browns 1-7.

But the real memory was November 14, 1999, in Pittsburgh. This time, it was Phil Dawson kicking a 39-yard field goal with no time left on the clock for a stunning 16-15 victory over the Steelers. Palmer could have called a timeout. Maybe he even should have called a timeout. But he wanted to make sure that field goal attempt was the last play of the game, and the Browns barely got it off in time. But they did. And they won. Palmer had put the picture of the ball going through the goalposts for that winning kick on his office wall. This game was treasured by the fans, too. The Browns had lost the previous seven games in Three Rivers Stadium, the last victory in Pittsburgh being 51-0 in 1989.

How many years in a row did we have to suffer at Pittsburgh, many times with us having a better team? And here was a new team struggling so badly and they willed themselves to win on a late FG into the wind. My brothers and I jumped and screamed as if the Super Bowl was ours.

—Matt Nahodil

Lipstick on my jersey, that's how I'll always remember that game! I've never been more emotional in a game of the new Browns than that one. We were so starving for a win and to have it come against the Steelers—in the last minute? Awesome! In the celebration after the game in the seats, somehow in all the hugs and kisses some lipstick ended up on my jersey. I didn't wash it off for quite a while.

—Jeff Williamson

All I could think was, "Wait, the clock! Wait, the kick! No timeouts left? Wait, where's my heart medication? Wait, I don't have a heart condition. Yet!"

—Barry Grey

The remarkable part of Palmer's tenure was a 2-2 record vs. the Steelers. The first home victory . . . it didn't come until 2000 . . . also was against Pittsburgh, 23-20. Problem was, Palmer had a 3-25 record against everyone else. He also was assuming that he'd be around for most of his five-year contract.

"If they had told me that I had two years, I'd have drafted Ricky Williams and played Ty Detmer," Palmer said. "I would have pushed to sign as many veterans as we could and then I'd have played them. We could have made some trades for veterans. It also could have turned into a Carolina situation, where you win in your second season, but after that, you don't have much for the next few years."

Carolina was 7-9 in its first year, 12-4 in Year Two. But in the next three seasons, the Panthers were 19-29 and bottomed out at 1-15 in 2001. They regrouped and went to the Super Bowl three years later.

And Carolina had 478 days to assemble a franchise, compared to 155 for the Browns.

What's the point?

The Browns were put together quickly and poorly.

Palmer and Policy did not seem to be on the same page, or Policy changed the page and Palmer wasn't aware of it. Palmer still denies it, but it didn't take long for there to be a split in the front office. Policy, Clark, and others who had been with the 49ers were in one camp, Palmer in another. It was very clear if anyone was going to take the fall for what happened in the first two years of the team, it was not going to be any of the San Francisco imports. Palmer had a 5-27 record in his two seasons. He was a rookie coach and made mistakes. He also didn't have much help from the front office. At the start of the second season—remember, the Browns were 2-14 in 1999—Policy said in a press conference that he thought 7-9 was a realistic goal and the playoffs were not out of the question.

I remember calling Palmer right after that pronouncement. He was stunned into silence for a painful moment. Then he carefully said he appreciated Policy's optimism, but the team had a lot of work to do. But he was upset. He knew that Policy was setting him up for failure, unless the team had a remarkable turnaround.

11. A Good Guy Takes the Fall

> These are not my Browns. I can tell you what I was
> doing during the 1964 Championship game, and I still have
> the transistor radio that I listened to the game on. So I
> have been a fan for a long time—good, bad, Bernie and
> Belichick. These are not my Browns. I can't put a finger on
> as to why, but it just isn't the same. So when is the next
> game on?
>
> —Kim Watkins

The expansion Browns were born into a dysfunctional family.

They had money. They had some good intentions. They had every financial and physical need met. But they didn't have a real leader, a true wisdom figure who could express a clear vision for the team, and then make sure it was carried out.

Al Lerner hired and trusted Carmen Policy.

Policy hired and trusted Dwight Clark.

Clark hired and trusted a lot of scouts, many of them from the 49ers.

Policy and Clark hired Chris Palmer, but never seemed to really have full faith in him.

In the end, the Browns wasted money, draft picks, free agent signings, and cap room during those first two years. How much of this was Chris Palmer's fault? I don't know. Would Chris Palmer have done as well as Butch Davis in

Years Three and Four of the franchise? I don't know that, either.

I do know that Palmer had a miserable second season, at least after the first three games in which the Browns were 2-1. They beat the Bengals in Cincinnati, the Steelers at home. I'm not even going to rehash the old hash that became the rest of the season. It was a year when about everyone got hurt. Couch played only seven games as he broke a thumb on his throwing hand in practice. After he delivered a pass, his hand banged into a teammate's helmet. Detmer had limped off during an exhibition game in Chicago with a torn Achilles, and he was done for the season. Browns fans then were relegated to watching Doug Pederson and Spurgeon Wynn play far more quarterback than they ever should in the NFL. Eric Rhett was supposed to help the running game and he did early, but broke his foot on his 71st carry of the season. Travis Prentice ended up being the team's leading rusher, and he's now long gone from the NFL. Rhett never came back from his injury.

I just remember Palmer's last game. It was a snowy December afternoon on the lakefront. Every breath from Palmer's mouth was a puff of white smoke. The teams should have been led onto the field by dogsled. It was a cold, bitter, frozen stretch of ground looking about as hopeless as Palmer's situation.

For weeks, I knew Palmer was done.

I knew it the moment Palmer said, "Sometimes, I feel like I'm driving a runaway train. In the first two seats are the owners. In the other two seats are the personnel people, and then the coaches and the players are in the back. And everybody's saying, 'Stop the train! Stop the train!' and you don't have time to tell them, 'Hey, we can't slow down. We've got to keep going.' "

I knew it when they lost 48-0 in Jacksonville and never crossed the 50-yard line.

I knew it because I talked to the man every week and I could tell that the front office (mostly Policy) was distancing itself from the coach. I knew it because this is what happens to most coaches of expansion teams, and it was why Brian Billick was so interested in Baltimore. It's why several coaches told Policy, "I want to be your second coach." It's what I see too often in sports and life: Some of the best people get the worst breaks.

I watched Palmer on that brutally cold Sunday, the worst weather in his two seasons coaching the Browns. I wondered if he was thinking the same thing, that this was a lousy day and a lousy way for a job to end. He later told me that was not the case, that he was fixated on the game, trying to win— which wasn't going to happen.

He was playing Rahim Abdullah, who had been in some discipline trouble at Clemson and had question marks next to his name for attitude. He also was considered a physically gifted underachiever. I know this was a Dwight Clark pick, especially in the second round, because Palmer loathed players with this kind of baggage. At one point in the season, Abdullah told some reporters, "I'm gonna vote for Bush."

Too bad the election had been two weeks earlier.

Hate to think about how he prepared for a game each week.

Many fans don't remember the thin talent or hurried start that hampered Palmer, just the "runaway train" line.

"Bill Parcells used that line all the time," Palmer said in the spring of 2004. "What happens is once the season begins, you can't make a lot of changes. In pro football, you make the changes in the off-season [with the draft, trades, free agent signings]. But once it starts, that's it. I was on Bill's staff when another coach was saying that this player was no good, that player was no good. Bill interrupted and said, 'Hey, this is a runaway train and you better understand that because there is no stopping it. What we've got is what we've got, and nothing is going to change it.' That's all I was trying to say, but I think some people heard that and thought I was saying things were out of control."

That's exactly how it sounded to many members of the media and to many fans, especially given the disastrous season. This also points out a mistake made by many coaches—which is quoting or imitating another coach. Parcells can say things like that because he has won Super Bowls and no one doubts that he is in command of whatever team he happens to be coaching. But Chris Palmer did not have Parcells' credentials. Bill Belichick alienated many fans and members of the media while in Cleveland when he was sarcastic and arrogant in press conference, much like Parcells. The difference is no one does Parcells better than Parcells. Belichick has fared much better in New England simply by being himself—rather boring, but polite. Many media members used to complain about Palmer's bland press conferences, until they spent three years with Butch Davis. Suddenly, they looked back fondly at Palmer, saying, "At least Chris was being honest."

That may have hurt him with some members of the front office and fans.

Palmer once was a special education teacher. He's a man with a loving father's heart of patience. He spent two years telling fans, "This is all part of the process." He talked about "managing the game," which sounded like he was afraid to play to win. He said he believed the best personality on the sideline was "flat-liner," no emotion. He was criticized for that. Of course, Ohio State's Jim Tressel is the same way. The difference is Tressel wins, Palmer lost.

After the 2000 season, Palmer met with Lerner, Clark, and Policy.

According to Palmer, Lerner asked, "How many games can we win next year?"

Palmer said, "I think we can win six."

He looked at the faces in the meeting and realized his answer—the straight one—was not what they wanted to hear. He explained that he thought they could make the playoffs in the fourth year. But he realized no one was listening.

"I didn't want to have a situation where I said we'd win nine games, and we won only six," he said. "Especially when I didn't see us doing that, not if we wanted to continue to develop the young players. Butch came in and they won seven games, instead of six. Which is about the same in my mind. In the fourth year, they made the playoffs. I knew they were losing confidence in me. I heard they thought my practices were too hard, which is why we had so many injuries. The irony was they hired a guy whose practices are harder than mine. Everyone knows Butch Davis runs very physical practices. Look, they can spin it any way they want, it doesn't necessarily have to be true."

Policy should have fired Palmer right after that meeting. But they didn't and part of Palmer wondered if perhaps he would survive. Maybe he was thinking back to earlier in the season when Policy "guaranteed" that Palmer would be back and Lerner said it would be a "travesty" if Palmer wasn't given another chance.

Policy said he knew Palmer was done after two years.

"There was a point in that [2000] season when I knew we had to make a change, and this was before I even thought about Butch Davis," he said. "We were headed in the wrong direction. Al [Lerner] liked Chris Palmer and was convinced Chris came into a bad situation. But I told Al, 'We need to change the environment, or we'll just keep doing the same thing.'"

Lerner told Policy that he thought Palmer deserved another season, but if Policy thought he could find someone better, they could make a move. That began one of the most inexcusable chapters in the history of the new Browns. For several weeks, Palmer remained the coach, yet the media was full of reports of Policy courting Butch Davis, who had just coached the University of Miami to a No. 2 national ranking. Palmer's friends in coaching were telling him that they heard he was finished. The media was holding his professional funeral, but Davis supposedly was close to signing a new contract to stay in Miami—yet his agent was still talking to the Browns.

You know what happened.

Palmer was fired, Davis was eventually hired. But why they made Palmer wait for all those weeks during the courtship of Davis is a question even Policy can't answer. In his rambling press conference to announce Palmer's firing, Policy at one point said he wanted to retain Palmer "to see if he finally gets it." Then a few moments later, he said he had "lost faith" in Palmer's leadership in the middle of the season.

Palmer had signed a five-year, $5 million contract. He was going to be paid all of it, despite coaching only two years. But that is why a coach has a contract. Yet at the press conference, Policy took a cheap shot when he said, "Chris is the kind of guy who would coach for nothing and he'll be able to coach for nothing after this contract."

In the statement Policy released to the press, he said,

"Chris Palmer believes we don't have a problem, that everything is fine . . . don't worry about problems that don't exist. Don't worry about looking for changes, because changes aren't necessary. I believe that he believes that. . . . That's where the disagreement came in. I respectfully submit to you, as I respectfully submitted to Chris Palmer, that it is my opinion, we do have problems . . . we are not on the right track."

That statement makes it sound as if Palmer thought his 5-27 record in two years was acceptable, which he did not. And that Palmer believed there was no reason to upgrade the roster, which was outrageous. He told the front office the type of players they needed to improve. He made recommendations for the draft, and he had targeted Ladanian Tomlinson as the first pick.

"We needed a running back, I thought Tomlinson was going to be a star," Palmer said. "If we had a shot at him, I wanted to take him. I worked on the draft until my last day on the job, even though I had a pretty good idea what was coming."

You can disagree with everything written here about Chris Palmer, but few fans would doubt the man's character or dedication. Chris Palmer may not have been a great coach for the Browns, but he was entitled to more respect than that from Policy. There are better ways to fire someone.

"When Carmen called me to say I was being released, someone in the front office had already contacted the media and leaked the news to one of their buddies," Palmer said. "I really resented not being told first. I had tremendous respect for Al Lerner. I love Browns fans. I still get Christmas cards from them down here in Houston. My family was as happy living in Cleveland as anywhere we've lived. It's a great place. I want the Browns to succeed because the fans deserve that.

I knew it was going to be a tough job, but I was 49 years old and it was my first chance to be a head coach in the NFL. I had to take it. I then took the first bullet, and there were others fired later. Instead of everyone staying in the same boat and rowing together, some people were saying, 'It's all HIS fault.' Division from within conquers marriages—and sports teams."

Palmer looks back at Policy's history with the 49ers and believes his old boss didn't grasp the challenge in Cleveland.

"I know there were some lean years before Carmen got to San Francisco," he said. "Bill Walsh was the rock that the franchise was built around. They [Policy and Clark] weren't there in the beginning when things were real tough. They reaped the benefits of [Walsh's] hard work and staying the course. . . . Sometimes, when you get in at the tail end of it and you haven't rolled up your sleeves from the beginning, it may seem easier than you think."

A lot of my Browns memories come from watching the games with my dad. It brought us closer together. We'd talk about Bernie Kosar and Webster Slaughter during the game. Even though the [new] Browns stink, it still brings my dad and me together. It's an excuse to hang out and have father/son bonding. With me going to school and working, it's hard to spend time with him. The Browns bring us together for three hours. I look forward to going to a bar and watching the game with my dad as we discuss the good and mostly bad things that the Browns are doing.

—Bryan Rejkowski

12. New Man in Charge

There are three things about the Browns:

1. There is no helmet logo. This implies a mystique about this franchise unlike any other before or to come. Why?

2. Because they are named after a man. An important man in the history of the league. Paul Brown. His history, his tradition of innovation and excellence should be continually celebrated, honored, and followed.

3. There is no dome, no artificial turf. Why? Because Cleveland Browns Stadium is a venue for how football is meant to be played.

—Joe Hertzel

It seems the Browns have been looking for the next Paul Brown ever since Modell fired Brown . . . or at least since the retirement of Blanton Collier after the 1970 season. Modell once defended Belichick's personality to me by saying, "Hey, Paul Brown was no walk on the beach, either."

Carmen Policy wanted his own Paul Brown, or at least a coach who was a name, a coach who would be an instant hit with the fans. He found one in Butch Davis. Apparently Dwight Clark also thought Davis was a great idea, at least for a while.

About a week before Chris Palmer was fired, Clark appeared in Palmer's office.

"Did you hear the rumor?" Clark asked.

"Dwight, if Butch Davis comes here, not only will some-one else be sitting in my seat, but there will be someone in your seat also, because he's not coming unless he has total control," said Palmer.

Thinking back, Palmer added, "Dwight looked at me as if to say, 'Geez, I never thought of it that way.' Butch had total control at Miami, so why would he leave Miami to go some-where else unless he had total control."

Palmer's point was valid. Why would Davis leave his little empire in Miami unless he could rule the Browns his way? And why should he trust his future to Clark, who was put-ting together a regrettable track record with the Browns? And what choice did Policy have but to give Davis what he wanted?

Policy was desperate. Davis is a tremendous recruiter and salesman, which is why he will always be a successful college coach. He oozes confidence. He says all the right things with conviction. He makes you want to believe him. He has a per-sonality that immediately earns him respect and attention, at least in the short term. Policy believed the Browns were floundering under Palmer, and wanted a coach who would clearly be in charge.

Davis definitely was that man.

Policy had no one to blame for this mess but himself. He turned the team over to Clark. His insistence that he couldn't entice an experienced GM to take the job is an indication that Policy either didn't try hard enough, or lacked the manage-ment and recruiting skills to convince someone to take the position. Obviously, Lerner had the money to pay to anyone whom Policy deemed worthy.

As for Palmer, in the end, he was Policy's hire. First choice or fifth choice, Palmer ended up with the job. To Palmer's credit, he never blamed Clark for his failure. In several lengthy discussions in the spring of 2004, he said that he and Clark agreed to make Tim Couch and Courtney Brown the first-rounders in 1999 and 2000. He said they agreed on Dennis Northcutt and Kevin Johnson. He did admit that Rahim Abdullah "was not my kind of player." But he insisted that he worked well with Clark and respected Clark's sincerity and dedication. Palmer added that he was weary of the Davis regime blaming Clark for everything that has gone wrong since.

But Davis has a right to be disillusioned by the team he inherited.

The Policy/Clark regime had 28 picks in the first two drafts. The expansion Browns were given bonus selections at the end of each of the seven rounds. Football is a sport where a Pro Bowl player can be found in the middle rounds, and occasionally as non-drafted free agents. It's not like pro basketball, where the vast majority of star players are high picks. Good scouting and a little luck should have given the Browns far more than what their first two rounds produced.

Consider the following:

- Only one player from the 1999 draft was with the Browns at the beginning of the 2004 season, that being starting corner Daylon McCutcheon, a third-rounder. The Browns cut their first two picks—Kevin Johnson and Tim Couch. Johnson is now with Baltimore, a useful player, but not a great one. Their other second-rounder, Abdullah, is long gone from the NFL. There were no gems uncovered in the lower rounds.
- In the 2000 draft, the Browns had the top pick again. They went with Courtney Brown, who remains with the team, but the only season Brown played all 16 games was his rookie year. When it was over, Clark said Brown

was "spectacular . . . if I could pick a Courtney Brown every year, sign me up." Brown did appear ready to become an impact player, then came the endless injuries.

- Dennis Northcutt was the second-round pick in 2000, and probably is Clark's best decision. He has speed and can be very effective returning punts. He was the team's leading receiver in 2003.
- As the 2004 season began, McCutcheon, Brown, and Northcutt were the only players left with the Browns from those first two drafts. Johnson and Couch were elsewhere. Of the remaining 20 players picked, none were starters, and 17 were out of the NFL or on practice squads.
- The Browns didn't pick a single offensive lineman in 1999, and only two in 2000: Brad Bedell (sixth round) and Manuia Savea (seventh round).

How did the Browns operate in the first two seasons?

"They basically were controlled by a committee, with Carmen Policy having the final say," said Palmer. "It was basically a combination of Dwight, Joe Collins [a scout], and myself. Al Lerner and Carmen would talk to Dwight and myself and ask whom we wanted in the first round. Dwight and I both agreed on Couch and Courtney Brown. Carmen really didn't get involved in the football decisions; he relied on Dwight Clark for information. Carmen and Al Lerner would come in sometimes to watch films and I'd try to explain to them what was going on. In addition to coaching the team, I was spending some time telling those guys what we were trying to do."

Palmer defends the picks near the top of the draft, as those are the ones where he had the most input.

"Northcutt and McCutcheon are good players," he said.

"Courtney looked like a very good player, but the injuries . . . Kevin Johnson has been a very productive player in this league. We got Shaun O'Hara as a free agent out of Rutgers, and I think he has become a very useful player for a kid who wasn't even drafted. As for not drafting linemen, offensive linemen do not score points. You have to get yourself to the point where you can put points on the board because it's the only way to win in this league. You try to build a line with guys taken in the fourth, fifth, and sixth rounds."

The early Browns put a lot of free agent money into their offensive line, signing veterans Dave Wohlabaugh, Orlando Brown, and Lomas Brown, and taking a $2 million player in Jim Pyne in the expansion draft. By the middle of the 2000 season, Pyne had blown out his knee and would never be a viable NFL player again. Orlando Brown had been hit in the eye with a penalty flag tossed by an official, the kind of freak, one-in-a-million event that seems only to happen to the Browns. The big tackle was out of football for several years until his vision came back and he returned to the NFL with Baltimore in 2003.

"We don't have much to show for all those picks, the situation speaks for itself," Carmen Policy said. "I didn't make the picks, but this has to stop at my door. Looking back, I sense we didn't have a real plan in place. We put too much reliance on what we were hearing from other people instead of the innate ability of our key evaluators to go out and work and judge and decide where players fit."

Browns fans can get a migraine if they spend too long studying the missed opportunities.

Some fans are critical of the Browns picking Courtney Brown in 2000, especially since Lavar Arrington has become a star with Washington. Policy told me that the Browns considered trading that top pick in 2000, "but we really didn't get an offer for it. We went with Courtney because he was a defensive end, and it's supposed to be harder to get a great defensive end than a linebacker—but we really liked Arrington, too."

Policy paused.

"If there ever was such a thing as a blue-chip draft choice, Brown was it," he said. "He had character. He had never been hurt in college. He had tremendous ability. Every coach who ever had him just loved him."

The bottom line is, seldom has a team ever had so many high picks and ended up with so little to show for it.

Butch Davis said he wasn't aware of the problems that he inherited when taking over the Browns.

Nor did he care.

"Before I was hired, I didn't look at any tape of the team, I didn't even look at a media guide," he said.

Really?

"I knew eight to ten of the players," he said. "That was it."

Davis told me this on a snowy Christmas Eve in 2003. Former *Beacon Journal* football writer Pat McManamon and I spent nearly two hours in his office as he gave us his state of the team. He had graphs and charts prepared to show the dismal state of the Browns, especially the poor drafting and free agent signings during the Clark era.

"You look at this, and you realize Chris Palmer never really had a chance," he said.

"So why did you take the job?" I asked.

"Because it was one of only 32 head coaching jobs in the NFL, and I really liked Al Lerner and Carmen Policy," he said. "I knew Al had the resources to be a great owner. Carmen had run teams that went to the Super Bowl. He had been on the big stage. I knew the fans loved football in Cleveland. It was a place with no divided loyalties, everyone was a Browns fan. It wasn't like when I coached at Miami and the state was divided by Florida, Florida State, and Miami fans. Here, it's all Browns."

This gives an important insight into Butch Davis: He doesn't fear he'll fail, even in the most difficult circumstances. The Browns are a popular franchise with a dedicated, wealthy owner, a new stadium, and a tremendous fan base. That was enough for him to believe he could transform them into a winner. No one believes more in Butch Davis than Butch Davis. He'll never say it, but he thinks he's a great coach. He thinks his way is the right way. He thinks that given enough time, he'll win. Egotism? Of course, but all the elite coaches have the same unwavering confidence. That spirit is what attracted Policy. He wanted a charge the hill, plant the flag on top kind of guy. He longed for a coach who was the boss. He needed someone to tell him, "Don't worry, Carmen, we can get it done here."

Policy was desperate.

Davis was looking for a new challenge. In the back of his mind was what he had done at Miami. The Hurricanes were in serious trouble with the NCAA when he arrived in 1995. They were losing scholarships, at one point playing with 20 fewer scholarships than the NCAA limit of 85, a disaster for a football program attempting to compete for a national title. Sports Illustrated proclaimed the program a cesspool that should be shut down, given the death penalty by the NCAA. Some of his friends advised Davis not to take it, but he did. And he brought Miami back to the doorstep of the NCAA title. He also did it with minimal problems with his players and graduation rates in the 60 to 70 percent range most years.

Davis not only won, but even his detractors admitted he did it the right way, bringing order out of a crisis situation. When there was a discipline problem—as is often the case with major college football programs—he handled it well. Davis was the perfect man to revive the Miami program.

So he was not intimidated by anything he heard about the Browns.

Instead, he thought back to his days with Jimmy Johnson at Oklahoma State, at the University of Miami, with the Dallas Cowboys. In each place, things improved once they arrived. He often talks of being 1-15 with Johnson in their first season with the Cowboys in 1989, and how the team went on to win Super Bowls in 1992 and 1993.

How much worse than 1-15 in the football hotbed of Dallas could it be for him in Cleveland?

Besides, if you're Butch Davis, you don't much worry about what happened before you arrived. You just figure you'll find a way to fix it. You have done it before, you'll do it again. You do it with the power of your personality, the knowledge that you've gained, and your personal history of success and beating the odds. You're smart. You don't want to play for a nutcase or cheapskate of an owner. You won't let anyone be your boss and dictate which players you'll coach. You know there have to be certain things in place, and the Browns had them thanks to Lerner. You don't think about the 5-27 record in the first two years. In fact, if you're Butch Davis, you consider that to be a positive. This miserable team won five games in their first two years? How can I do any worse than that? There is nowhere to go but up. No matter what I do, it has to be better than what has been done before.

The Browns?

If you're Butch Davis and they are offering you a five-year, $15 million contract with complete control of the football operation . . . you figure you can't lose.

"I knew I needed a significant voice in the football operation," he said. "I didn't care about the marketing and the business parts, but I wanted a voice in football—much like Jimmy Johnson had."

Policy gave it to him.

"I always admired Butch going back to when he was a defensive coach in Dallas," said Policy. "I was impressed with how he handled Charles Haley. When we [the 49ers] traded Haley to Dallas, Butch somehow managed to turn him into a good citizen. Haley helped get them to the Super Bowl, and Butch deserves credit for that. Our [49ers] coaches were always impressed by Butch's defenses when he was there. I had talked to Jimmy Johnson over the years and he was always high on Butch, and this was long before I ever thought of hiring Butch. Then I looked at what Butch did in Miami and I was convinced that he wasn't just a good coach, he was able to put together a plan and see it through."

Clark lasted 15 months under Davis, then resigned quietly. He really did work hard. He desperately wanted to prove himself. The Browns were a chance to revive his career as an NFL executive after being blamed for the decline of the 49ers. He just couldn't pull it off in Cleveland.

Now it was Davis' turn.

"I had no thought of hiring another GM," said Policy. "Butch had a reputation for having an eye for evaluation. He had sent a lot of guys from Miami to the NFL. Besides, if we had tried to bring in a GM, Butch would not have come."

Davis received everything he wanted from the Browns.

"The ultimate for a football coach is to win a Super Bowl in the most competitive level of football," he said. "That's why I came to Cleveland."

It's also why Davis didn't study the details before accepting the offer. The power to pick players, the money, and the length of his contract were signs of commitment. If you study the history of NFL coaches who eventually led their teams to the Super Bowl, Butch Davis seemed to come to the Browns with the proper pedigree. Heading into 2004, there were 39 coaches who took their teams to the Super Bowl.

Twenty-five of the 39 had played on an NCAA or NFL championship team, or served as an assistant for those teams. Twenty-three had been involved with teams as players and/or assistant coaches that won more than one championship.

Davis fits this profile. He's been an assistant under Jimmy Johnson at the University of Miami when the Hurricanes were the consensus No. 1 team in the country in 1987. They also were ranked No. 1 by some polls in 1986 and 1988.

Davis then followed Johnson to the Dallas Cowboys, where they won two Super Bowls.

Finally, he served as a head coach at the University of Miami when the Hurricanes finished No. 2 in the country in 2000, although some experts believed they were the best team in the nation.

It was hard to argue with Davis' résumé. And when he came to Cleveland, no one did argue. He was greeted like the football savior. He looked good, sounded good, and his last Miami team had played great. He had been exposed to the NFL under Johnson. More than a few NFL executives thought he'd be the next Jimmy Johnson.

The Browns were counting on it.

13. Butch & Big Money Cost the Browns

It has been pumped into my blood that you root for the Browns, through thick or thin, until death do us part. One reason is I remember what it was like not to have a team. It was horrid. No one would dare to root for Cincinnati or Pittsburgh. The Browns are a part of who we are in northeast Ohio. When holidays come, people get together and talk, play games, watch TV. When you live here, each Sunday is a holiday when the Browns play and we watch the games. We are a family, not always happy, but neither are other families. We always hope next year will get better, hope that one day we will make it past The Fumble and The Drive. We hope we finally will get a draft pick that's not a waste—a coach who actually can make us a good team, year after year. We fans hold onto a hope that a better team will come, hopefully sooner than later. Bark!! Bark!!!
—Michael Kager Jr.

There's hope.

That's what most Browns fans said during the first year of Butch Davis.

There's hope from a new coach with a big name and a personality that screamed he was in charge, so everyone just relax. There was hope from yet another draft with yet another pick, this time being the No. 3 selection in 2001. There was hope because underneath all the growling and whining from Browns fans, there's always hope.

The Butch Davis Show was all about hope.

But that didn't stop Davis from messing up the 2001 draft.

According to a couple of sources who were involved in that draft, the Browns seemed to be set to select defensive tackle Richard Seymour. At least some people in the room believed that had been the verdict. But on the day of the draft, Davis supposedly changed his mind—and went for Gerard Warren. This surprised more than a few people that day. Davis says all his major decisions come from input from those he respects, hours of discussion, and research. That may be true. But in the end, Davis made his pick, and it was not even close to a consensus of the men doing the draft. This would not matter if Warren had become a player worthy of the No. 3 pick in the draft.

Instead, it became the first—and not nearly the last—example of Butch Davis the general manager making life tough for Butch Davis the coach.

When Gerard Warren was mentioned, someone should have told Butch, "Hey, in Cleveland, you just don't pick a guy whose nickname is Big Money!"

Especially when he acts like a Big Money.

I'm going to spend some time on the thought process that led to Big Money coming to the Browns, because this was the first significant decision made by Davis. It also was a costly one. If Davis had drafted Ladanian Tomlinson, life as a Browns fan would be so much better today. This was the choice of Chris Palmer. He was a player several scouts insisted would be a Pro Bowl running back. He was a player the Browns needed, and Davis had been bemoaning his new team's "inability to run the football."

Had the Browns simply picked Tomlinson, two major things would have happened:

1. They would have had a great running back since 2001.

2. They would not have had the heartache of William Green, the back they drafted in 2002 because they failed to take Tomlinson in 2001.

On the day of the 2001 draft, the Browns did not even mention Tomlinson during their various press conferences.

"Butch was going defense," said Policy in the spring of 2004. "Tomlinson was not on the table."

Who was No. 1 on their board when it came time to make the third selection?

It was Michigan's David Terrell!

Who is David Terrell? He is a receiver for Chicago, the No. 8 pick in that draft. He has been so-so, catching 43 passes (one for a TD) in 2003. He's no better than Quincy Morgan, so the Browns caught a break when they passed on this athlete, who also had a history of stress fractures in his foot. Dwight Clark was still around for this draft, now doing the type of job that Policy said he first pictured for the former 49ers receiver. He was helping Davis, who was the GM/coach without that official title. At the draft day press conference, Clark said the Browns rated Terrell at the head of their overall draft list of available players. They had another list—players to meet needs. Warren was No. 1, according to Davis. Others had Seymour ranked ahead. Maybe there were two lists, or maybe some people are engaging in revisionist history. But Warren's strongest advocate was the man whose voice mattered the most.

Want to feel even worse?

Ozzie Newsome had the No. 31 pick in that draft, the last in the first round after the season in which his Ravens won the Super Bowl. Newsome grabbed a tight end named Todd Heap, who has made two Pro Bowls. Newsome has had 11 first-rounders since taking over the Ravens, and seven of them have become Pro Bowl players. He is an All-Pro tight end turned All-Pro general manager. Not every pick he makes is a bull's-eye, but he rarely misses the entire target.

Meanwhile, back at the Browns camp . . .

It was obvious that Butch Davis was an inexperienced NFL general manager, and it showed in his first draft.

Why pick Big Money?

"To win football games, you have to run the ball and stop the run," Davis said on draft day. "Teams draft for years and never come up with guys that dominate the line of scrimmage. He is the kind of guy you just couldn't pass up. Having coached several defensive linemen in college and the NFL, we felt Gerard came close to, and is in the same category as, Cortez Kennedy and Jerome Brown."

Another comparison was later made to Warren Sapp, this one coming from Big Money himself.

Clark went with the company line, saying Warren was "a franchise-type defensive tackle . . . a nasty, violent player . . . the kind we need here."

Gerard T. Warren of Raiford, Florida, was 6-foot-4, 325 pounds of ego. Davis tried to recruit him to play at Miami, but Warren picked Florida instead. But Davis remained enamored of Warren, and wasn't bothered by Warren's arrest during his freshman year on marijuana charges that led to a two-game suspension. To be fair, more than a few college students have gotten into trouble with marijuana, and many have matured and not had problems since. A more alarming rumor about Warren was that he "took plays off." His own coaches said Warren needed to play hard every game to attain his enormous potential. This was no secret. You could find it in any pre-draft report available to fans and media. At a press conference about a month before the draft in which he talked about the various players available, Davis defended Warren, insisting that the tackle "fights you on every play."

As a fan, you've been watching Warren for three years— you decide what was the most accurate scouting report.

As I look back at what I wrote from draft day, I'm embarrassed. Part of me knew they should have picked Tomlinson. I was bothered by the charges that Warren could be an underachiever. Did I address any of this? Nope, I was bowing at the altar of Butch Davis. The theme of my story seemed to be if Butch picked the guy, then that's all right with me. Here's a condensed version:

> The drafting of Gerard Warren is a signal that the Browns have one loud, clear voice in charge of this team. A voice that belongs to new coach Butch Davis, as it should. Not to team president Carmen Policy, who probably would have loved the Browns to pick a sizzling running back . . . or a game-breaking wide receiver. Not to Dwight Clark, who said Michigan wide receiver David Terrell was their highest-rated player in terms of pure physical gifts. Not to anyone else in that room who might have had another brainstorm. This was Davis' first major decision, and it's refreshing that he was allowed to make it.
>
> Defensive tackles aren't sexy. They don't sell tickets. They seldom bring fans out of their seats. "All they do is help you win games," Davis said.
>
> Like Jimmy Johnson, Davis appears to have an eye for talent. Consider that four of the players he recruited at Miami were picked in the first round . . .

> But the real story on this day is as much Davis as Warren. It's that the Browns finally have one man in charge, and it's about time.

This from a guy who has always believed a strong general manager is the key to building a winning franchise in any pro sport. And this from a guy who had doubts about Warren. This from a writer who decided to hitch his wagon to the Butch train, in much the same fashion as Policy. I should have known that any player called Big Money since high school probably has some issues, especially when he sometimes refers to himself as "Money." Big Money picked up the nickname in high school, because friends said he'd one day be making the big money in the pros. That has indeed come to pass, so the prediction was right. But Warren has yet to prove he's right for the Browns. Now we can see that eight players taken after Warren in the first round became Pro Bowl selections.

The 2001 draft was supposed to be THE YEAR OF THE DEFENSIVE TACKLE. Five of them were picked in the first round—and three have been Pro Bowlers. Warren is one of the two that has yet to reach the lofty expectations set for him. Meanwhile, defensive tackles Richard Seymour (No. 6 to New England), Marcus Stroud (No. 13 to Jacksonville), and Casey Hampton (No. 19 to Pittsburgh) have all been to the Pro Bowl. So have three running backs: Tomlinson, McAllister, and Minnesota's Michael Bennett. Add in guard Steve Hutchison (No. 17 to Seattle) and Heap (No. 31 to Baltimore) and you wonder how the Browns could have missed drafting a Pro Bowler at No. 3—but they did.

The second round wasn't much better as the Browns turned to Quincy Morgan, a big, fast receiver from Kansas

State whose reputation was that of a natural athlete who didn't always run his patterns correctly and had unreliable hands.

Let's stop right here and examine the first two picks of the Davis regime, which do tell us much about the man running the Browns. They also were indications of what was to come. Morgan and Warren have much in common. They both have tremendous God-given physical attributes. They are fast. They grade well in areas where pure athleticism is measured. But both were considered somewhat underachievers in college. Both were the kind of players that Davis saw and said, "Hey, we can get these guys to play the right way, we'll just coach 'em up."

The 2001 draft was where they picked Jeremiah Pharms in the fifth round, and the linebacker never even made it to camp as he was arrested on serious felony charges and sent to prison. The Browns tried to dismiss this, as a fifth-round pick is pretty much a gamble, anyway. Yet they kept Tim Couch in limbo for months trying to squeeze a fifth-rounder out of Green Bay or another team. And the fifth round in 2002 is where the Browns found starting middle linebacker Andra Davis. The Pharms fiasco was an indication that someone didn't do their homework—or didn't care that he had some character issues that turned out to be more serious than they ever imagined.

Warren has started every game but two for the Browns, but his immaturity showed. He was benched for the Cincinnati game during his rookie year because he was arrested for having a handgun in his SUV. Several people in the vehicle had marijuana, although Warren did not face any drug charges. Davis acted quickly, saying the conduct was not acceptable. Carmen Policy then spoke, adding that he had talked to the officer in the Pittsburgh area who had busted Warren. Big Money was at a mega-party thrown by a member of the Steelers, and Policy said the officer told him, "Gerard was the nicest guy he ever arrested."

Now there's a ringing endorsement!

Anyway, Warren returned from the suspension to play the best football of his first three pro years. In the last six games of the 2001 season, he averaged nearly eight tackles, had three sacks, and was the force in the middle of the line that the Browns imagined. But in 2002 and 2003, he never approached those standards, averaging slightly less than four tackles per game—half of his output in those six games after the suspension. Did he have six All-Pro games because he was embarrassed after the arrest? Or was it just a fluke? Was it because blockers began to pay more attention to him after that, and he often was double-teamed? Did the Browns' defense schemes change?

All of these explanations (rationalizations?) were offered at various times in the last few years. The bottom line is, Warren has not measured up to what a team should expect from the No. 3 pick in the draft, or what he showed he could do in the final six games of his rookie season. At the end of 2003, Davis was defending the pick, insisting only "two or three guys have better stats" when playing the same position as Warren.

Warren has had some effective moments, but no consistency. He may be a better than average defensive tackle capable of playing a great game occasionally. He also has confessed to not taking football seriously, to spending too much time on parties and the ladies—his terms, not mine. A few times, he has said he's ready to grow up, has learned from his mistakes, and a new, improved Big Money is on the way.

Warren often says all the right things, but doing them is a different story. It's a shame that Butch Davis the general manager had such a mediocre first draft, because Butch Davis the coach had a very strong rookie year.

14. In Butch We Trust

It's the Good Years. The 1964 Championship. The Bill Nelsen Era. The Kardiac Kids. The Dawgs/Kosar Era. They were SO good, waiting for a new winning era is not that daunting. I need to be there when the Browns turn it around!

—Sheldon Green

I was at the rental car counter in San Jose when a friend called to say we got Butch Davis! I loved it! My friend sounded lukewarm. I was not. Butch was THE answer to my Super Bowl prayers. I told him that day: In Butch I Trust. Three seasons later: In Butch I Trust. The team he took over in 2001 had very few players who were going to be useful. Yes, he may have had a taller mountain than even he thought he'd have to climb, but he is decisive and sticking to it—regardless of what the fans and media think . . . I think Butch was learning the NFL system and still is . . . but he will make this team one to be proud of.

—Matt Edwards

Butch Davis wasn't Paul Brown, but he came to town as the man with a plan. He easily took command, and the influence of Clark and Policy quickly diminished. You could tell when Ty Detmer was traded for a fourth-round draft pick. Detmer was a former 49er, a favorite of both Policy and Clark, who wanted him to start that first season instead of Couch. Davis preferred free agent Kelly Holcomb, who was strongly endorsed by new offensive coordinator Bruce Arians. The 2001 team remains his best coaching job in his first three seasons. He took over a group that was 3-13 and had lost eight games by at least 20 points. In his first season, it was only two losses by at least 20 points. The team lost two in overtime, a total of four by a TD or less.

And Davis won seven games.

He even won three of his first home games, which is one more than in the first two years combined!

For a month, it appeared the Browns had a home field advantage. As for whatever happened to that, don't ask the Browns. None of us seem to know, other than Davis fielded a team in 2001 that was confident and immediately embraced by the fans. He gave them a taste of success. Maybe just a sip, but a few drops of water on the parched tongue of a heat-stricken, sandblasted man staggering through the desert often is enough to keep him going.

So it was with the Browns in 2001.

Davis deserves credit for delivering Browns fans a reason to believe. Not that a Super Bowl was imminent. Not even that the playoffs were certain. Not even a winning record was guaranteed. But the Browns became a team that kept fans watching most games right until the end.

They beat Baltimore . . . twice!

That was remarkable, because the Ravens were coming off a Super Bowl season. In the first two seasons, the Browns were 0-4 vs. Baltimore, outscored 114-26.

When they upset the Ravens in Cleveland on October 21, here's a condensed version of what I wrote. It reflects how most Browns fans felt on that special Sunday in 2001:

Butch Davis rushing across the field, fist raised, fans cheering, wind whipping, sheets of rain pelting Cleveland Stadium.

Tim Couch carrying the football as if it's his first-born child.

Drenched fans who were complete strangers at the start of the afternoon slapping palms like old friends.

So this is what it feels like to beat the Super Bowl champions. This is the day when Browns football really returned, the day when some new tradition was made.

Browns 24, Baltimore 13.

It was a day when the Browns went shoulder-to-shoulder, bruise-to-bruise, block-to-block with what's supposed to be the meanest, nastiest, most arrogant team in the NFL.

And they never flinched.

In the end, the Browns didn't just beat the Ravens, they beat 'em up.

Or as Davis said, "Our defense was just relentless. It was suffocating. They spilled their guts all over the field."

Not a pleasant image, but football guys love that kind of talk because it's the ultimate compliment. It means every step, every hit, every play was contested. Helmets cracked. Pads crunched. Bodies banged.

This came after a disappointing 24-14 loss at Cincinnati, where the Browns were out-hustled in addition to out-played. Last Monday, Davis was angry, wired, determined. With his jaw out, he was challenging his players to regain their passion. He was insisting to the media that the Browns were ready for Baltimore, ready for anyone. He was serving notice: The past is buried, this is a new Browns team.

And it sure was yesterday: From Tim Couch throwing key

TD passes to gutsy calls by the coaching staff, to determined defense.

"Right now, we're a little battered, a little beat-up, a little bruised," said Davis.

But feeling no pain.

Davis did change the culture that year. His defense played so aggressively they were fun to watch. In the next two years, I wondered what happened to that mindset. In that first year, Davis had a perfect understanding of what his team needed: a coach who didn't want to "manage" the game, but win it. A coach who seemed to play fearlessly. A coach who didn't have much to lose, because all the team had done was lose. So what if the blitzes didn't always work? So what if some of the gambles failed? So if what they lost, at least they went down fighting! That was what Davis told the team.

It worked, especially in the beginning.

They went to Baltimore and won again . . .

I sounded like the team's press agent:

Are you falling in love yet?

I mean, with the Browns?

Do you understand that none of this should be happening, that the new Browns are creating their own tradition each week? That Butch Davis should be Coach of the Year, if they handed out the award today? Or that Tim Couch took a horrible beating, yet kept bouncing back, shaking off the bruises, the bungles, and the interceptions to show that maybe Davis is right when he says, "Couch has the kind of heart that one day can lead us to the Super Bowl."

And speaking of hearts, is yours beating a little faster as you think of what the Browns did in Baltimore yesterday?

Final score, 27-17.

Wonder how Art Modell's breakfast tastes this morning? Bet those Corn Flakes are soggy, the rolls like lumps of coal, the coffee tastes like battery acid.

His team has lost—what?—TWICE to the Browns?

Now Davis has the pros playing like kids.

Fun.

Over and over, you hear that word from the millionaires in the Browns locker room. This game is fun. This season is fun. These guys are fun.

Ain't it the truth?

And I wonder if anyone—except Mr. Positive, Butch Davis—would have expected the Browns to give us this kind of season. His team has made the games Must See TV every Sunday afternoon.

That was a game where Ben Gay came out of nowhere— and soon to return, by the way—to score on a seven-yard sweep. He had another 21-yard dash in which, according to what I wrote, "he shook off two tacklers, stepped on a third and stiff-armed a fourth before he was dragged down from behind. Oh, I forgot to mention how he spun like a top to shake off a tackler on another memorable run, too."

Ben Gay didn't last. The Browns found out there were reasons why he couldn't stick out college, why he failed in the Canadian Football League. It can be summed up when he said: "Christmas is a great holiday, it just comes at the wrong time of the year."

Sort of like Rahim Abdullah planning to vote for George Bush two weeks after the election. You don't have to be a genius to play pro football, but a sense of reality does help. That was absent from Gay, who had tremendous physical blessings but lacked the discipline to take advantage of them.

A player who does have a clue and who may end up being the best of the 2001 draft is Anthony Henry. In that Baltimore victory, the rookie defensive back had three interceptions. A guy named Devin Bush ran an interception back for 43 yards and a TD. But the Browns intercepted a lot of passes that year, a league-high 33 to be exact. Here's an interesting statistic: You take those 33 interceptions in 2001, and then realize the Brows only totaled 32 interceptions in the 2002 and 2003 seasons combined.

The reason is they stopped playing with the same abandon. That often happens when a team suddenly thinks it is supposed to win. The Browns did not have a good defense in 2001, but they had an exciting one that allowed 100 fewer points than the year before, moving from 27th to 15th in the league.

But in the next two seasons, they usually played boring defense, and they were not much better.

After the Baltimore game, the Browns were 5-4. Then on the same night, Gerard Warren was arrested on a gun charge. Tight end O.J. Santiago was arrested on marijuana possessions charges. Starting H-back Mike Sellers was arrested (in a different city) on drug charges. Davis suspended Warren for a game, and immediately cut Sellers.

But this was an indication of what was to come—Davis' players have legal troubles. Go back to fifth-rounder Jeremiah Pharms being jailed before he could even get to training camp, and you have two draft picks (Pharms and Warren) and two veterans (Santiago and Sellers) who were busted that first season. But Davis seemed in control, especially when the Browns beat the Bengals, 18-0, the next week—and they did it at home.

At this point in the season, the Browns were 6-4 overall, 4-2 at home.

On December 16, the Browns made national news. Not because they finally had become a viable football team, but because of bottles. I'm not going to spend much time on this story. A few thousand out of 72,000 fans began heaving plastic bottles onto the field after the officials blew a call that probably cost the Browns the game. Officials even allowed the Browns to run another play, then overruled. It was a mess. The crowd was cold, more than a few of them drunk, and it rained down bottles. It was a sickening, embarrassing display. After the game, Davis handled it with expertise. He said most fans were not at fault, but too many got out of hand. He said he was "disappointed," and wanted Cleveland to be known as a "first-class city." He added that bottle-throwing "puts our players in jeopardy, as well as their players."

Davis should know. I was on the field as the second wave of bottles came down. Davis limped past me. I asked what happened, and he said, "Bottle got me in the knee."

The Browns should have been thanking God that nothing serious came of this. Instead, the front office—Carmen Policy and Al Lerner—made excuses. They simply should have echoed the comments of Davis. Most fans were not throwing bottles, but even one of them is too many. They planned to make sure it didn't happen again, and to help law enforcement officials find the violators.

How hard is it to say the right things?

Plenty, if you were to listen to Policy and Lerner that day.

I now give Lerner a free pass for this. I now know that he was already being treated for brain cancer, and that he never should have been brought into that situation.

There is no rationalization for what Policy said. "They are plastic bottles," he rambled. "They don't pack much wallop."

His bottom line?

"I'm not condoning it, I'm just not criticizing it," he said.

The national media took this as an endorsement of drunken behavior, and Policy not only embarrassed himself, but the team and the fans. The next day, he had to apologize for the remarks at yet another press conference.

Most of the time, I find Policy to be a very intelligent guy with more than his share of common sense. But he sometimes thinks admitting a mistake is worse than the mistake itself. He was trained as a defense attorney, and he sometimes still wants to debate every piece of evidence, even when there is no debate. It's fact. Bottles flew. Fans and football people were hit. There are no excuses.

Which is what I admired so much about Davis in 2001 . . . he was a man without excuses. Once again, the Browns led the league in injuries. As Palmer predicted, Davis' practices were even more grueling. As Palmer said, "When you have a young team, you need to be in pads a lot in order to learn. You need to be on the field. You don't want the guys to kill each other, but they have to practice what you are teaching them."

Davis agreed. After peaking at 6-4, the Browns were wearing down. The team would win only one more game that year, but it was an amazing game. They went to Tennessee on December 30, 2001. They were on a four-game losing streak. Here's my story:

> Just when you think the tank is empty . . .
>
> Here comes the Browns—again.
>
> The Browns who came to Tennessee with 19 players who weren't even on the roster at the beginning of September.
>
> The Browns who had lost their last four games, whose quarterback was in a slump and whose playoff dreams had been

broken. These Browns were down by 14 points early in the fourth quarter against the Titans. These Browns, whose best offensive lineman [Ross Verba] was too sick to play. These Browns, whose defense just seemed too tired after carrying the team for so long.

These Browns appeared to be finished.

Or at least, that was true of the old Browns, the Browns who were 5-27 in their first two expansion years. But these are the Browns of Butch Davis, the world's most positive man. These Browns beat Tennessee, 41-38, by scoring 17 points in the final 9:21 of the game. That's 17 clutch, fourth-quarter points from a team that hadn't scored 17 points in any of its last four games.

These Browns are different.

These Browns are coached by a man who told kicker Phil Dawson, "We're gonna have the wind at our back in the fourth quarter so you can win the game with a 44-yard field goal."

Davis spoke it, and it happened.

Said it at HALFTIME, when there was no way to even guess. And said it was 44 YARDS, not 40 or 45 yards.

And Dawson heard that, nodded, and thought, "Sounds good to me."

So here it was, 55 seconds left in the game. Score tied, 38-38. On the field comes Phil Dawson, the smallest Brown, who is generously listed at 5-foot-11, 190 pounds. Little Phil Dawson jogged onto the field, the game resting on his toe, the ball to be set up at the 34-yard line. With the uprights 10 yards deep in the end zone, that made it a 44-yarder . . .

Just as Davis said.

With the wind at his back . . .

Just as Davis said.

And yes, Dawson made it. Couch set it up by throwing three TD passes and racking up 337 yards in the air. In the previous six games, Couch had three TDs compared to 13 interceptions. It was then that Davis said, "He can take this franchise to a place it's never been before."

The Browns finished that season at 7-9, but full of hope. Davis could have run for mayor, but never would have considered it because coaching the Browns seemed like a more important job at the moment.

Next year?

Davis wanted the playoffs. The fans believed he could take the team there.

15. A Playoff Mirage

I was born with burnt orange in my veins. I know
nothing else. I still wear my Browns coat that is about 15
years old. Quite warm and still in good shape. I'll probably
be buried in it. I'll have at least one Browns item in my
coffin. It's hard to explain why I continue to be a Browns
fan even after they left for Baltimore, and all the bad
seasons, blunders, and mistakes. It's what being a fan
is all about. True fans don't change allegiances. Being a
Browns fan is inbred. It's living and dying with each pass
and interception. Never giving up and waiting until next
year with the excitement of a child on Christmas. I love my
Browns. I wear my colors with pride. My cubicle at work is
decorated with Browns gear all year long. I cried when they
left. I read the franchise agreement when they came back,
every page. I have pictures and posters, hats and pins and
license plates. Yes, and coats, ties, and socks. Why am I
a Browns fan when it still hurts? It's part of us. It's what
we'll always be and it's who we are.

—Tony Lowe

I'd take my son to Lakeland Community College each year
for training camp. I have pictures of him reaching up to
give High 5s to Clarence Scott and Thom Darden. I think
that's what got him hooked. One summer, I had won an
official NFL football. My son took it to camp looking for

some autographs. The only one he got that day was Bernie Kosar, who seemed to be the only player signing. But that was fine because he's our all-time favorite Brown. I'm 57 years old and now live on Long Island. Since the Browns have come back, my son and I come to one game each year. We drive out on Saturday, then back to New York on Monday. Being with all those fans tailgating in the parking lot can't help but make you proud of being one of them. It's one of the highlights of our year.

—Chris Brown

Know what 2002 was for Browns fans?

A taste of the playoffs that turned bitter. Fans now know that. But how many of us realized it was a mirage, that 2002 was not a year to build upon? It was a tease. It was not what Carmen Policy talked about when he said the original plan for the franchise was three years of building, a playoff appearance in Year Four, and contention for the Super Bowl in Year Five.

They made the playoffs in Year Four, but took the now-infamous "step back" in Year Five, that phrase also belonging to Policy. The 9-7 record in 2002 followed by 5-11 in 2003 shows you that the Browns still had a long way to go—and that Butch Davis still had a lot to learn.

Here's one lesson: In the 2002 exhibition season, Jamir Miller ripped an Achilles tendon and never played for the Browns again. After the first five years of the expansion era, Miller remains the only Brown to make the Pro Bowl, and that was in 2001. Part of the reason the Browns had so many interceptions that year was Miller chasing quarterbacks, forcing them to make poor throws to avoid a sack. Davis claimed Miller's 13 sacks were more "the product of the system" than

Miller's ability. That was where Davis' ego obliterated common sense. It also was a lack of respect for what Miller had accomplished. The players knew it and didn't appreciate it. Davis understandably didn't want the Browns to pout and feel overwhelmed by the loss of Miller. But it was a mistake to insist their pass-rushing linebacker was nothing more than a body on the football assembly line—and anyone else standing in that spot would be equal to the task.

The players who replaced Miller at linebacker did not have a single sack that season. In fact, five different men shared time at the three linebacker spots, and they combined for four sacks—nine fewer than Miller in 2001. Davis wants his team to believe it can overcome anything. That's admirable. But he sometimes crosses the line into territory where it sounds like the coach thinks he can fix anything—and anyone. The Miller situation is just one example.

Consider Davis's 2002 draft where the first-rounder was William Green. Most fans know his story. He is a running back from Boston College. He lost both parents to AIDS when he was in junior high. His father was a Vietnam veteran who contracted the disease because of his drug use. He then infected Green's mother. One of the coaches who became close to Green when he was in high school later was arrested on child molesting charges. He never hurt Green, who continues to support the man. But just imagine the feelings of abandonment that have been a part of Green's life. He attended Holy Spirit High School in Atlantic City, New Jersey. To Green's credit, he went to one high school and to one college—Boston College, a good one. He seemed to be searching for stability. Green was a fabulous running back in high school, rated as the third best tailback in the nation by one well-respected recruiting service. At Boston College he was a star, named the Big East Player of the Year in 2001. Butch Davis knew Green well, at least William Green the running back. Since Miami and Boston College are both in the Big East, Davis watched Green not only on the field—but in depth on film as he prepared to coach against him in those games.

When the 2002 draft came along, Davis knew a few things:

1. The Browns were dead last in rushing.

2. William Green would probably be available.

3. Green had been suspended twice for marijuana use. Once for a bowl game, and once for the Miami game.

4. Green was not a violent young man, but he was troubled.

5. If William Green stayed straight, the Browns could have a legitimate back for the first time since the team returned.

But what if he failed? What if there were more suspensions, more drug use? What if the pressure of playing for pay didn't take off the pressure on Green, but increase it? After all, many players coming into millions of dollars suddenly find they are expected to give massive amounts of money to friends and family—especially if they want to "keep it real" and "remember where they came from." Why do so many young men who turn pro find themselves in a financial squeeze? It's not only because they spend wildly on themselves, but they also hand out money to countless relatives, friends, and leeches now appearing in their lives. A player can receive solid guidance from a respected agent, excellent advice from financial planners, and encouragement from the team to be shrewd with his money. But too many young pros can't resist the temptation to pay for things they don't need and people who don't mean them well. It's impossible to know how much of this was a factor in Green's situation, but people continually wanting cash from him is a fact of NFL life. Too often, teams and college players believe turning pro will make life easier.

It rarely does.

I still wonder how much the Browns thought about this before drafting Green.

"It was a crapshoot," admitted Davis a year later. "But in that draft, there were three to eight guys with alcohol, drug, and other problems."

That also is a fact of NFL life. Running around stadiums on NFL Sunday are so many damaged, struggling men who have come from a swamp of family mess and are trying to shake themselves free of their past. Besides, if the Browns had passed up Green and if he had continued to play as he did in the second half of his rookie season (averaging 105 yards per game), fans would now be screaming, "How could they not take him! They needed a back!"

That's why being a general manager is such a tricky job. How much risk is too much? In 2001, they gambled on Gerard Warren. Because the defense tackle finished strong, Davis considered that pick—his first pick—a grand success. He did not imagine Warren regressing as he did in 2002. When it came time to draft, Davis was confident in his judgment and drafting instincts.

As Policy said, "Everyone in our room agreed Green was the best back in the draft. If he had a background like Lee Suggs, he goes in the Top 10. We made a decision based on need."

It was also based upon Davis saying he could handle the situation. So he used the No. 16 pick on Green, who was the first running back selected.

Now, fans say, "Why didn't he pick Clinton Portis?"

I heard no one say that on draft day. Portis attended Miami, where he played for Butch Davis. It appears their relationship was somewhat rocky. Portis went in the second round to Denver, where he gained more than 1,000 yards in each of his first two seasons.

"If I took Portis, then everyone would have been down my throat for taking a Miami guy," Davis told me. "Portis is one of five runners to gain over 1,000 yards in the last 10 or so seasons in Denver. It's the system. I don't know if he does that with us."

Davis has been criticized for drafting players with Florida ties, either those who played for him (James Jackson, Andre King, Joaquin Gonzalez), or players from that state such as Warren (Florida), Anthony Henry (South Florida), and Andra Davis (Florida). But two of his best middle-round picks of the new era have been linebacker Davis and cornerback Henry, so this argument is not always accurate.

It doesn't matter where the players come from, it matters that they can play.

And when he's right, William Green can play.

He ran for 887 yards and was named the Browns' 2002 MVP. But remember that Gerard Warren had his best performance in the second half of his rookie season, just as Green did. After that, Warren tailed off.

Green fell off the sobriety wagon and was arrested and suspended in 2003. He played only seven games, and that's a big reason the Browns fell apart one year after being a playoff team.

Some fans have said Warren and Green are the same type of people. Not so. Green is a much harder worker. But both had drug issues in college. Some teams worry about this.

Two player personnel directors told me that they would not have picked Green in the first round, that he was too much of a risk. He simply had too much baggage. It's a real concern when a player knows he will be drug tested, yet was caught smoking weed during the weeks of two of his biggest games in college. This does not sound like something casual, or at least that was how these executives from other NFL teams saw the situation. Davis and his staff checked out Green, interviewed Green, liked Green personally. They correctly say that a lot of players in the draft have legal issues . . . drug issues . . . personal issues. Many come from disastrous home situations. Green's was more extreme than most, but not especially uncommon. In fact, more players now come from single-parent and/or broken homes than from the classic two-parent home.

The positive thinking that serves Davis so well as a coach can hurt him as a general manager. He believes he can deal with almost anyone, that they will adapt to his system, buy into his personality, trust his leadership. He hoped that would happen with William Green. Between 2002 and 2003, the Browns were 8-6 when Green started, and he gained 1,285 yards in those 14 games.

"He single-handedly turned our 2002 season around," said Davis.

And Green's fall from grace helped shut the 2003 season down.

Once again, Butch Davis the general manager hurt Butch Davis the coach with a questionable first-round pick. In the second round of 2002, Davis selected Andre Davis from Virginia Tech. This was the fourth consecutive year the Browns used a second-rounder for a receiver. That tells you that there's something wrong. It's like Davis knew his 2001 second-rounder, Quincy Morgan, wasn't the player he thought. So he tried it again with Andre Davis.

Here's the four receivers: Kevin Johnson, Dennis Northcutt, Morgan, and Davis.

It's not a bad group, but just suppose the Browns had drafted offensive linemen in the second round for those four years. Don't you think the team would be in better shape today?

In 2002, the Browns lost the first game, 40-39, to Kansas City. It was the helmet toss by linebacker Dwayne Rudd that cost them a victory, as he was celebrating what he thought was a game-ending sack. It wasn't. Rudd was flagged for an excessive celebration penalty. Kansas City was given one more play, and the Chiefs won the game. It also was a game where holder Chris Gardocki was flagged for taunting after Phil Dawson kicked what he thought was the game-winning field goal. Later, it was mentioned that the kicker Dawson . . . not holder Gardocki . . . was the guilty party. OK, but when was the last time you saw either a holder or kicker penalized for taunting? This game pointed to a weakness in Davis' coaching—his appeal to emotions. Chris Palmer was criticized for his players being too composed, and he was supposedly too under control as he coached from the sidelines. Now, Davis' players seemed out of control, with too many late hits, too much trash talk.

That remains an issue with his coaching.

But even more important are his decisions as general manager. He may not have realized it at the time, but the 2002 season rested with William Green. When the troubled running back rushed for at least 95 yards, the team was 4-0. When he didn't, they were 5-8, counting the playoff loss to Pittsburgh.

These Browns were a strange team. They made the play-offs, but in the process lost confidence in Tim Couch. There were several times when it appeared the Browns were out of the playoff race. Couch missed two games early in the season with a forearm injury. Kelly Holcomb replaced him. When Couch was healthy, Holcomb returned to the bench. In the same game where Couch went out with a concussion, Holcomb relieved and after the game discovered he had broken his leg. In the final regular season game, Couch broke his leg, but Holcomb was healthy enough to return. Somehow, Davis held them together. Remember, they'd lost their best defensive player in Jamir Miller. They had both quarterbacks injured. Courtney Brown missed the final four games with injuries. The turning point was after a 23-20 loss to Pittsburgh, followed with a bye week allowing Davis time to reassess the season, then regroup. The Browns were 4-5. Green had done little, the team seeming to have lost faith in the run. In fact, the pass-run mix was 64-36 percent, meaning they were throwing the ball nearly twice as often as they ran it. This was not in the game plan. In those last seven games, the mix was 50-50. They went 5-2. The defense got more rest (as the running game chewed up the clock) and allowed only 18 points per game.

In the final, must-win game, the Browns beat Atlanta, 24-16, a game where Green played like Leroy Kelly, galloping for 178 yards in 27 carries, including TD runs of 21 and 64 yards. He seemed all that was advertised, and more. Meanwhile, the 9-7 Browns had made the playoffs. Davis took a team that was 5-27, raised the record to 7-9, and then to 9-7. For that, he deserves a lot of credit.

Then came the playoff game against Pittsburgh, which not only meant so much in 2002, but set a disturbing tone for

2003. Most of you know the story. The Browns went to Pittsburgh on a snowy Sunday in January. They had already lost
twice to the Steelers, by three points each time. Couch was
out with the broken leg. The ball was in the hands of Holcomb, who had become the People's Choice. And you probably know the final score was 36-33 Pittsburgh. You may remember that the Browns had a 24-7 lead in the third quarter,
a 33-21 lead with 10 minutes left, but the defense couldn't
hold.

Here's my story from that game:

> So this is how it ends for the Browns, losing a game they
> should have won.
>
> It ends with Kelly Holcomb standing at midfield, watching
> the Pittsburgh players dance around him as he looked like a
> guy who just lost his date on prom night, right after renting
> the tuxedo. "I'm sick to my stomach," he said.
>
> It ends with Butch Davis throwing out his jaw, chewing on
> his lower lip and knowing he won't sleep well on this night.
>
> It ends with the Browns believing they should be alive in
> the playoffs, convinced that they are able to beat Pittsburgh.
> And it ended with the Browns running out of time, partly
> because they ran out of timeouts as they squandered all
> three in the third quarter. It ended with Pittsburgh scoring
> 22 points in the fourth quarter. It ended with Heinz Field
> shaking as fans stomped and screamed and celebrated as if
> they had just won the Powerball Lottery.
>
> It ended with this final score: Pittsburgh 36, Browns 33.
>
> Goodbye playoffs, hello quarterback controversy.

This was the game of Kelly Holcomb's life, as he threw for
429 yards, second best in Browns playoff history on a day

when the game-time temperature was 27, snow was swirling, the wind was whipping, and puffs of white vapor came from players' mouths. Holcomb did his best Brian Sipe imitation, and Butch Davis wasn't the only guy wondering if Holcomb should be the quarterback in 2003. So was I. So were many of you.

16. Strangers in Orange Helmets

Cleveland loves players who want to play for this city. We crave players who fight hard and give everything they have with no complaints. What separated Tim Couch from Bernie Kosar, Omar Vizquel, etc.? The supporting cast. I want Tim to know that not everyone holds him responsible for the tough times.

—Matt Nahodil

I'm not a Couch-hater, but let's be realistic. He was not the best player available in the 1999 draft. He was lucky to be picked No. 1 by the Browns. They were an expansion team and had to start somewhere. His career has been mediocre at best. I do feel he did the best he could for the Browns, and I can think of a few other ex-Browns QBs who were worse.

—Dan Abrigg

Couch was mishandled from the start. Management pushed the panic button after the slaughter against the Steelers and rushed him in with little or no chance of success. He never had the supporting cast to prove if he is anything other but average.

—Frank Loucka

I really liked Couch from Day 1 . . . the exhibition game at Canton. He is/was my favorite Brown. He'll be the guy I remember from the new Browns about 20 years from now. I think he got a raw deal and was never adequately supported.

—Kyle St. Peter

My son fell in love with the Browns when he received a Tim Couch uniform for Christmas a few years ago. He has since upgraded to an authentic Couch jersey. He wears it proudly to school daily, and we live in Pittsburgh Steeler territory. He cried for 15 minutes when I told him that Tim probably would no longer be with the Browns.

—Mark Mroczynski

Know why so many Browns fans still respect Tim Couch?

Who else was there? Who else was the face of the new Browns? Who else gave the team any identity? Close your eyes and think about the player who made you first love the Browns: Marion Motley? Otto Graham? Jim Brown? Leroy Kelly? Bill Nelsen? Brian Sipe? Ozzie Newsome? Clay Matthews? Bill Glass? Jerry Sherk? Greg Pruitt? Bernie Kosar? Reggie Langhorne? Earnest Byner? Frank Minnifield & Hanford Dixon?

Not all of them are Hall of Famers. A few may not even be considered great players.

But they were guys who mattered to us. They made us care.

Why do I love the Browns?
Toughness.
Bernie Kosar was one tough cookie for looking like such

a "college boy." Bernie got it done. Bernie was smart and tough, and Bernie was LOYAL. Fans don't forget that. Doug Dieken was just flat-out tough. He wore that toughness weekly. Ditto for Clay Matthews, I think he was made of steel. I'm proud of the Browns for their history of being a tough team. You might score more points off them at the end of the game, but you had to work your butt off, and maybe FREEZE and endure LOUD fans to get away with it. A win against Cleveland cost you something. Ask anyone who ever had to face Dixon and Minnifield. Again and again, I've been proud of this team. I wish the new Browns would convince themselves who they are and get an identity—in a word, it should be toughness.

—Dan Lebo

Lebo's letter makes a good point.

The Browns need an identity. They need players who are around long enough for the fans to know them, players who are good enough to bring some success on the field. Fans want a player to follow. Who else was there besides Couch? Courtney Brown can't stay healthy or on the field. So many others have come and gone. The 2002 Browns made the playoffs, but had no real identity. They were "a bunch of guys." That's what Couch said the team felt like in 1999, and in many ways, they remained that way.

A bunch of guys.

Just so happened that those bunch of guys had a decent year in 2002, finished 9-7. Kelly Holcomb had a career-game against Pittsburgh in the playoffs. In the quest to find someone to turn into a hero for the fans, Holcomb was presented with several commercial opportunities. He even had his own brand of barbeque sauce. Interestingly, that product was made in Pittsburgh, where his brief time as a starter also was born. But talk about desperation. Holcomb had started a mere three games for the Browns, and he was being marketed as a marquee player. And the quarterback who had an 8-6 record as a starter that year—and 7-3 down the stretch—was benched. An expansion team made the playoffs for the first time in its four-year history, but the coach wasn't sure who should be the quarterback. The defensive coordinator was fired. Several key veterans were cut for salary cap purposes. The team president warned that a "step back" might be needed.

And the billionaire owner also passed away.

If you're thinking, "This could only happen to my Browns," then you are indeed a real Browns fan.

As for taking a step back . . . 2003 was more like falling on their butts. It began in the off-season when the Browns cut veterans Corey Fuller, Dave Wohlabaugh, Earl Holmes, Dwayne Rudd, and Jamir Miller. Much was made of Miller being cut, but he had a major Achilles injury and could not come back to play for anyone. Davis was right, Fuller was losing ground as a regular cornerback, and after signing with Baltimore, he was used primarily in passing situations when extra defensive backs were on the field. Holmes signed with Detroit and started, Rudd went to Tampa. But both were just OK. The Browns had made a mess of their cap, and that led not only to these veterans being dropped—but the only free agent signing of any consequence was Barry Gardner, who was a reserve linebacker.

No matter how the Browns spin and who was to blame—Davis, Policy, or both—this was poorly handled. The draft was, at best, boring. And could be lousy, if second-rounder Chaun Thompson fails to develop as the Browns expect. Most teams had the kid from little West Texas A&M as the fourth-rounder, or lower. But the Browns were convinced they found gold under a Texas tumbleweed, and jumped at the chance to draft a physically gifted young man who was not ready for the mental demands of the NFL. And they passed up Ohio State's Mike Doss to do it. Making the Browns look worse, Doss started for Indianapolis at safety, while Thompson mostly played on special teams. Was Davis trying to make a point with Thompson, showing how he could outsmart the rest of the league? Or did he really find a jewel? Just like with Gerard Warren and William Green, Davis took a major gamble again with a high pick.

First-rounder Jeff Faine did start and do a decent job at center. The most interesting pick may be running back Lee Suggs, taken in the fourth round as insurance in case something happened to Green—and indeed, something did. Suggs would have been a first-rounder but needed shoulder surgery. He missed the first half of the season, but showed promise in the final game when he rushed for 186 yards at Cincinnati. The Browns also took a long-snapper named Ryan Pontbriand in the fifth round, which several draft experts thought odd—most long-snappers are signed as free agents, not drafted. But Davis said he needed a "good long-snapper so I can sleep at night."

That was about the only reason he had to rest in 2003.

For a while, Couch was the quarterback. Then Holcomb. Then Couch. Then Holcomb. Then Green was arrested on drunk driving charges and suspended . . . as well as stabbed by his fiancée (and mother of his two children) in a domestic dispute. Green played only seven games, but was still the team's leading rusher for the year with 559 yards.

Courtney Brown was injured . . . again.

The Browns led the league in injuries . . . again . . . the third time in four years.

The offensive line was awful . . . again.

The defense was flagged for having 12 men on the field . . . and still gave up a seven-yard run!

Holcomb broke his leg . . . the "teeny, weeny fracture," according to Davis . . . on a quarterback sneak, which is not easy to do. He missed a month.

The Browns were dismal . . . again.

Are we having fun yet?

If Green is an example of the fragile hold the Browns had on success, then Couch is the poster player for the franchise since it returned. Not just because he was the first player picked by the expansion Browns, but because of his five years of stops, starts, sputters, and stalls.

Want a scouting report on Couch? Consider this . . .

1. HE'S PRETTY GOOD: This occurs when he plays after being off for a while. He looks good, he makes the right reads, gets rid of the ball quickly, throws crisply, and moves the team. Suddenly, here's the No. 1 you thought you were drafting.

2. WELL, HE WASN'T BAD: This is the next game or two. He doesn't look as sharp, some passes are off target. He's having problems picking up the rush and doesn't get rid of the ball nearly as fast, so he gets hit. Maybe there's an interception, a fumble. But he played well enough to score a couple of TDs and maybe win ugly or lose close.

3. THE GAME WASN'T ENTIRELY HIS FAULT: Things start to go down the toilet. He completes a lot of short passes and even has a few good throws. But other than that, he's throwing behind receivers, or wide, or high. He hangs onto

the ball too long and gets hammered a lot. There may be a fumble, or a "what was he thinking" interception. But he completes something like 13-of-19 for 98 yards, and the game never seemed to get completely out of control.

4. HE STINKS!: This happens right before he stops playing again. He looks totally overmatched. He makes turnovers that make you wonder if he's wearing the wrong set of contact lenses.

—Geoff Beckman

Then the process starts all over again as Couch regroups and plays a couple of good games. It's why when I go back and read my stories from the Couch era, I'm as inconsistent as Couch at quarterback. I'm high on him . . . then I'm not. I'm blaming the lack of support . . . then I'm wondering why Couch doesn't make those around him better. I'm ready for Holcomb . . . then after a few games, glad Couch is back.

The more I watched Couch, the more I found myself on the same ever-changing page as Davis—thinking the Browns do need another quarterback. In so many ways, I was acting like a fickle fan.

And I didn't like it.

I just know that in my 27 years as a sportswriter, I've never waffled so much and flip-flopped so often on any player as much as I did Couch. I think that's because I was like a lot of fans. I believed Couch was a sincere guy, and I admired how little he complained in his five years with the Browns. I've never held the night of the 2002 Baltimore game against him when Couch was removed from the game with a concussion, and then took the fans to task for "cheering" when he left the game. He thought they were applauding because he was hurt. Rather, it was because Holcomb was coming in. He forgot the general rule: In most NFL cities, the backup QB is the most popular man in town—at least until he plays. Couch wept as he did his postgame interview.

> Many will never forget the Baltimore game and the
> ugliness that happened with a dinged Couch. Why did the
> Browns let him near a microphone, given the state he was in?
> —Bob VanVelson

I asked the Browns that question, and they said Couch wanted to talk, that he insisted upon it. But he'd just sustained a concussion and was frustrated by not only losing the game—but possibly, his starting job. In five years and hundreds of interviews with the Browns, it was the only time he said something really dumb, and it came after he was hurt. I never took it seriously. I don't think most fans did, although those who didn't like him seized the incident to say it showed he lacked toughness. But the one thing Couch had going for him was grit. He sustained a terrible physical beating in his five years here, and handled it with grace. His line was generally poor. Unless Green was functioning well, there was no real running game.

"It's like he was star-crossed," Davis once said, meaning it seemed the stars never aligned right for Couch.

Those who don't like Couch compare him to Mike Phipps, who was with the Browns from 1970 to '76. He was the result of one of the most destructive trades in team history, sending future Hall of Fame receiver Paul Warfield to the Miami Dolphins for the right to draft Phipps out of Purdue. But Phipps played far worse with better talent than Couch. He sat for his first two years behind Bill Nelsen and his aging, creaky knees. In 1972 he finally started, and over the next four years threw

35 TD passes compared to 72 interceptions! Couch looks like Otto Graham with his 64 TD compared to 67 interceptions in his five years with the Browns. But Couch does not appear anything more than average, no matter if you consider purely the numbers, or just watch him play. His arm is probably average, and so is his mobility. He doesn't seem like a shrewd Kosar-type quarterback capable of making up and executing plays with the mention of a snap-count or in the pressure cooker of a huddle.

Here's a list of quarterbacks who were top picks in the draft since 1980: John Elway (1983), Vinny Testaverde (1987), Jeff George (1990), Drew Bledsoe (1993), Peyton Manning (1998), Couch (1999), Michael Vick (2001), David Carr (2002), Carson Palmer (2003), and Eli Manning (2004).

It's too soon to know about Carr, Palmer, and Eli Manning. But what about the rest of the list? The only player who'd rank below Couch would be George in 1990. Couch is the Browns' version of Danny Ferry. Both had superb college careers in a system that highlighted their strengths and hid their liabilities. The difference is Ferry came to a contending Cavaliers team in the NBA's Central Division. It was hard for Coach Lenny Wilkens to find minutes for him, and still try to win every game. Later in his career, Ferry became a starter at small forward for the Cavaliers and San Antonio. While drafted high like a star and paid even higher, he was mostly a solid supporting actor, a guy who found a niche in the NBA by making outside shots, working hard in practice, throwing a few elbows inside, and having outstanding character. But he was a 10- or 12-point scorer in his best seasons, and nothing close to the promise that followed him to Cleveland from his days at Duke.

Danny Ferry was OK, Couch is OK.

But Butch Davis wanted more.

That's why he benched Couch for Holcomb at the start of 2003, and why I thought it was a good idea at the time. In fact, I wrote a column under the headline "Gut Feeling Says Go With Holcomb" two days before Davis announced that it was his "gut feeling" to open the season with Holcomb. Given Holcomb's collapse, I'm not sure what that says about either of us.

I believe 2003 was the hardest year for fans since the Browns returned. They were teased by the 2002 playoffs, let down by Green's personal conduct and suspension. Many pinned their hopes to Holcomb, but he proved to be what he's always been—a backup. Some fans thought Davis played Holcomb because "Couch was not Butch's guy." It's easy to fall into the trap, given the way Davis has bounced most of the players he inherited. But most of them deserved to be sent packing. But even Davis backers had to be wondering what was happening when Kevin Johnson was cut at midseason of the disastrous 2003—a strange, seemingly meaningless move. He landed with Jacksonville before moving to Baltimore in 2004. The excuse about Johnson not being a good blocker had most football people rolling their eyes. Johnson was cut because he didn't seem to be one of Davis' guys, and because he was not the game-breaking receiver that Davis likes. But he's still a pretty good player who was given away for nothing.

"From the time Butch Davis got there, any Palmer guy was a threat," Kevin Johnson told reporters. "Slowly but surely, he wanted to weed out all of Palmer's guys, so Couch had no chance."

Johnson is not exactly unbiased. He clashed with the coach, whom he thought never believed in him. After he was benched in Kansas City, he dressed before Davis finished his postgame remarks to the team. A few days later, he was cut.

After the 2003 season, the Browns produced a chart revealing that 28 of 50 players inherited by Davis were out of the NFL. Twelve were with the Browns, 10 on other teams. None were Pro Bowlers, few even start. Most of the departed players deserved to be gone.

Couch was a different situation. He was the guy who was supposed to be capable of leading the Browns "to places this franchise has never been before," according to Davis in 2001. Davis also said Couch was a player "you could build a team around." He drew a comparison to Troy Aikman, how Aikman was 1-15 and 7-9 in his first two years before developing into a premier quarterback. Davis also endorsed extending Couch's contract and giving him an $8 million bonus before the start of the 2002 season. Dwight Clark and Chris Palmer decided to make (and pay) Couch as the No. 1 pick in the 1999 draft; Davis then affirmed that decision with the new contract. When Couch was cut in June of 2004, much was said about him being overrated back in 1999. But Davis also was wrong about Couch, and had completely changed his mind within a year. He watched Couch during all of 2001, and then agreed to the lucrative extension. By the end of the 2002 season, he was ready to switch to Holcomb. After the 2003 season, Couch was finished and Jeff Garcia was brought in as the new quarterback.

As the 2003 season dragged on, I asked myself, "If I were a young Browns fan, who would be my favorite player?"

I couldn't come up with anyone other than Couch, and he received the nod because of his simply surviving five years.

After Couch, then who?

Young Andra Davis plays with zeal at middle linebacker,

but 2003 was his first as a starter. William Green? Gerard Warren? Quincy Morgan? Daylon McCutcheon? A stronger case can be made that the best player of the expansion-era Browns was punter Chris Gardocki, and he was cut after 2003 because the Browns didn't want to tie up more than $1 million of salary cap money for a punter.

The Browns either had players who were bland, or troubled. In 2003, Warren got into a shouting match with his own defensive backs in an exhibition game. He was ejected for fighting during the loss at Seattle. He overslept for a meeting the day before the Baltimore game, and didn't start. The Browns also had a locker-room brawl between Robert Griffith and Quincy Morgan.

Baltimore's Jamal Lewis ran for an NFL record 295 yards against the Browns, but in his bizarre press conference the next day, Davis talked about how Lewis averaged a mere 2.4 yards on 25 of his carries, but had 235 yards on five other attempts. People asked themselves, "Is he trying to say the Browns did a good job on Lewis?"

This was like former Cleveland Indians manager Dave Garcia, who'd say things like, "Except for those eight runs we gave up in the third inning, it was a close game!"

To compound his penalty of excess spin, Davis then mentioned that defensive end Kenard Lang and Warren had "the best games" since they came to the Browns. If that was the case, why did Lewis set a rushing record?

Davis may have been trying to raise the sagging confidence of his defense, but to the fans it sounded as if the coach thought they were idiots—or that Davis had watched some other game. These and some other overblown statements hurt his credibility with the people who buy tickets and expect not only an honest effort—but a degree of honesty from the team.

The 2003 season seemed to shake Davis. He couldn't decide how he wanted his team to play. He said some ill-advised things, from reducing Holcomb's fracture to "teeny, weeny," to insisting the team was "on schedule" when it was on its way to 5-11. He later told me that he meant he was pleased with the development of some of the young players, not the record. It would have been wise to make that clear to the public, because it sounded like he thought no one was paying attention to the games. Fan backlash was sharp, and it was his fault. He was overwhelmed by all the injuries, especially on the offensive line. He told me how "the offensive line has been the curse of this franchise."

He revealed how the Browns spent so much and received so little in return: Roman Oben ($4 million), Jim Pyne ($2.5 million), Dave Wohlabaugh ($4 million), Orlando Brown ($4 million). Davis probably made a mistake when he cut Oben before 2001, as he went on to start for Tampa Bay's Super Bowl team. Davis said there were 423 players drafted and the Browns didn't take a single offensive lineman until Brad Bedell (sixth round) and Manuia Savea (seventh round) in 2000, but neither gave the Browns much. But Davis did not load up on linemen, either.

"Where do you start?" he asked. "When I took over, there were so many holes. We needed help at every position."

Before the 2003 season, the Sporting News ranked the Top 100 players in the NFL. Not a single Brown was mentioned. Naturally, the team was upset, claiming they had just made the playoffs and someone should have been on the list.

But at the end of the 2003 season, Davis and Policy were both talking about the team's "lack of impact players." They were hoping newly signed Jeff Garcia and/or top pick Kellen Winslow could change that. But how this franchise can be heading into its sixth year and still be mostly a bunch of faceless men under those storied orange helmets is why so many fans were sad to see Couch leave. He may not have been great, but at least he was someone they knew.

17. Needing a Reason to Believe

I still remember Red Right 88, and how that made me feel. I still recall the adrenalin rush I had with those same Kardiac Kids every week. I cherish the Kosar vs. Elway battles, even though we came out on the short end with The Drive and The Fumble. See what I mean? The Browns are just not whatever product happens to be wearing orange helmets in any given season.

—Tim Radwany

The Browns are a part of my psyche. The plays, the players, the memories, the traditions. The Browns have become a part of me, part of my soul, part of my family. Win, lose or draw, I watch them with the pride (and sometimes horror) of a father watching his sons play.

—Eric Bullock

Many of us are not blue-collar workers ourselves, but we come from working-class backgrounds where sports are our main hobby, our outlet for raw emotions, frustrations, joy and love. Both of my grandfathers were Browns fans. They loved Paul Brown and hated Art Modell for firing him . . . but still remained Browns fans. They worked in the steel mills and the Browns were an outlet. My father was the same way. The greatest gifts from him were Browns tickets. I just finished watching some old home movies.

It was Christmas morning, and both my brother and I had on Bernie Kosar jerseys. I feel great for the rest of the day when the Browns win, and physically sick when they lose. But I'd rather have that sick feeling than no feeling at all on Sundays.

—Justin Dublikar

For the past 16 chapters, you have been hearing Browns fans pour out their hearts about what this team means—and then reading about the mess that the team has been since it has come back. At some point soon, this has to change. In the five years since their return, it seems easier to memorize the entire IRS long-form tax code than it does for the Browns to win a miserable home game. Sure, they are an expansion team. But that doesn't explain the 11-29 record at home compared to 15-25 on the road. It appeared Butch Davis was changing that when he won three of four home games in his first season, but since then Davis is 6-14 at home heading into 2004. The Browns have the worst home record in the NFL since 1999, and they were 2-6 in 2003, so it's not just a product of expansion.

Know what this book is saying?

The fans still care, but the team needs to shape up.

Management has done almost the impossible—dulled the passionate loyalty. The team has been so thoroughly unlikable. They lose at home all the time and often turn in their worst performances in the games that matter most to the fans. . . . I also want to rant that the new stadium is sterile, ugly, phony, noisy, too steeply pitched, an overcommercialized, obnoxious piece of junk.

—Ed Cohen

The present regime is running out of excuses and the fans are running out of patience. Like the buzzards to Hinckley, the fans will continue to come to the lakefront. But if Randy Lerner and Butch Davis want our dinero, they better start putting up some Ws.

—Jim Galler

Most Browns fans have had moments . . . weeks . . . seasons . . . where they have been just plain mad. The first five years haven't shoved them into apathy, but it is driving them nuts. They want someone to believe in, a player to pull for, a team that feels like their Browns. The strangest part of this story was how the early Browns were an attempt to create the San Francisco 49ers-East. Ownership may deny that, but with Carmen Policy as the CEO, Dwight Clark as the GM, other former 49ers as scouts and players, and the fact that former 49ers coach Steve Mariucci was supposedly one of Policy's prime targets to coach the team, just what were they doing here?

No matter what he says, Policy thought the 49ers way was the best way—and the only way he knew. He decided to give the players virtually every perk imaginable. Barbers were brought in to cut hair. Cars were washed and detailed. Clothes were cleaned. Baby sitters were arranged. Travel was planned, dinner reservations were made. The best training camp food, the best of everything was available. The players were treated like Super Bowl champs.

If they had won, then you'd say they rose up and played to expectations. Also, this royal treatment was supposed to attract free agents.

But none of that happened.

A theory is the players already had everything, so they lacked the desire and fire to excel and achieve. But I don't think the problem was the players being spoiled as much as the players not being talented. The heart of the matter was poor management.

When Carmen Policy resigned in the summer of 2004, he knew that he had come up short. He also knew that he did not have a close relationship with Randy Lerner, at least compared to the bond Policy had with Al Lerner. And as one Browns insider told me, "Dwight Clark and some others suggested that Carmen hire John Fox or Marvin Lewis when he was courting Butch Davis. But Carmen didn't want to take a chance on another assistant coach who had never been a head coach before. He also thought Butch would be a name and stir up the fans. But in the end, Carmen created his own Frankenstein as Butch became more and more powerful. Butch cultivated Randy, and Carmen felt like a third wheel."

You can decide how much truth there is to that take on events, but once Al Lerner died, it was evident that Davis' influence increased and Policy's voice wasn't as strong. Give Policy credit for realizing it was time to leave, and doing it with grace. But the Browns still have so much more to do, besides just winning games.

> I hope the Browns hire some alumni so there is a connection to the past. I would like it to be Bernie Kosar because I believe he has strong character and integrity and I believe that's what the city is all about. If not Kosar, how about Felix Wright, Brian Brennan, Hanford Dixon, Mike Pagel, or any of the other former Browns still in the area.
> —Tim McNulty

Browns fans couldn't care less about the 49ers, or the 49ers way of doing business—especially since there was no

Bill Walsh, Joe Montana, or Steve Young doing it. When fans complain to the front office about wanting former players involved, it seems to confuse them. They may point to Doug Dieken in the broadcasting booth. OK, fine, who else?

Think about the Cavaliers. They have Austin Carr on TV and in the community. Former Cavalier Campy Russell also has a major position in community relations. Joe Tait never played for the team, but he has been their voice dating back to 1970—and in the eyes and ears of many Cavs fans, he is the team. The Indians have former players everywhere. Eddie Murray, Joel Skinner, and Buddy Bell are on the coaching staff. Charles Nagy and Mike Hargrove are "special advisors" and are around the team. Rick Manning is in the broadcast booth.

Baltimore has Ozzie Newsome as the general manager, with native Clevelander and former Browns player Pat Moriarty as Newsome's salary cap expert. Former Brown Earnest Byner is director of player development. Director of player personnel Phil Savage was with the Browns. Former Browns defensive back Bennie Thompson is an assistant coach. The Ravens still have far more of a Cleveland flavor than the Browns.

The Browns say they have done more for their former players than most teams. They supply free tickets to games. They have special buffets available. They have started their own ring of honor, and former players are showing up more often at halftime ceremonies. That is progress. But there were no former Browns players with a significant role in the organization until Paul Warfield was hired as a scout and player relations consultant. It's inexcusable that it took nearly six years for someone such as Warfield to be invited to join the front office. You'd think longtime Clevelander Al Lerner would have known better, even if this escaped Policy. But nothing was done, and it's what really bugs the veteran fans. Maybe Bernie Kosar doesn't want to leave his Florida home to commit full-time to work for the team, as the front office claims. But there are other players around. Don't you think a bright guy like Warfield (who has been successful in business after football) could have brought something to the Browns from Day One? He was part of another group that tried to get the franchise, so he obviously was interested. You don't just hire a former Brown to say you have a former Brown, but there are a lot of very talented former players who would bring a lot to the team. Find a couple and give them jobs that mean something.

They finally took some other positive steps, adding Jim Brown as a consultant and honoring the 1964 championship team during the opening weekend of the 2004 season. But that's just a start.

What about the new stadium?

"When we win, we rarely get a single complaint," said Policy. "It's only when we lose that we hear about the stadium. But when we lose, the lines are too long, the beer isn't cold enough, the stadium lacks personality. Well, it's the team that gives the stadium personality. People say the new stadium is not as loud. That's because they haven't had much to cheer for at home."

Some fans complain because they think the security is too strict, or because they can't bring a shirt or a banner that says bad things about the Pittsburgh Steelers. But these are minor gripes. Basically, Policy is right: the stadium will feel like a winner when the Browns begin to win. A fan doesn't need to be roaring drunk to enjoy a game, although more than a few Browns fans keep telling me the new team has driven them to taking a few sips of Old Panther Juice to ease the pain.

The problem is not the stadium, especially if the Browns can keep their ticket prices at the level they were in 2004, which was in the lowest third of the NFL. That's hard to believe, given what it costs to attend the game, but the NFL has been getting away with gouging fans for years, and the Browns are not even close to the worst offenders. Fans complained about the Permanent Seat Licenses (PSLs) when the team returned, where they had to pay for the right to buy tickets—and then purchase season tickets. But they bought PSLs, more than 50,000 at anywhere from $250 to $1,500 each. Then they bought tickets and there's now a waiting list of 2,500 people wanting season tickets.

> The fans who call the radio shows and insist they'll give up their tickets after the latest loss still have the passion to call, to vent. They will be there next Sunday, because it's in our blood and it always will be. We'll have a man on Mars before you figure out why.
>
> —Mark Kruse

A couple of fans sent me the following jokes, which were making the rounds on the Internet in 2003:

Q: What do you call 47 people sitting around a TV watching the Super Bowl?
A: The Cleveland Browns.

Q: What do you call a Cleveland Brown with a Super Bowl ring?
A: A thief.

Q: Why doesn't Akron have a pro football team?
A: Because Cleveland would want one, too.

Browns fans love this stuff. Part of them expects to suffer. Complaining is a form of bonding. The only humor seems to come straight from the football gallows. Many fans will enjoy this book just because it tells them what they already know—they've been getting a raw deal. Art Modell was a lousy businessman who stuck himself with a crummy stadium, then betrayed his loyal customers by moving to Baltimore. The NFL left Cleveland open so other teams could threaten to move and wrestle new stadium deals from their cities. The league then gave the Browns the third shortest start-up time in modern NFL expansion history. The new ownership turned the team over to Carmen Policy, who put an overmatched Dwight Clark in charge. Draft picks were wasted while overpaid, underachieving free agents were signed.

Then Butch Davis took over, and he was ill equipped to be both coach and general manager. The ideal situation would have been a strong, experienced GM helping Davis as a rookie coach in the NFL. But that didn't happen, and probably never will as long as Davis remains. He rejected Policy's attempts to have the respected Ron Wolf serve as a consultant, and the former Green Bay GM resigned after a few months of not being treated seriously by Davis. Some fans sense it's Bill Belichick all over again. He's learning on the job and will really figure it out the next place he coaches.

Browns fans may have an impending sense of doom about the team. After all, the team has won only four playoff games from 1970 to 2004, in the era of the NFL/AFL merger. Even the best memories are bittersweet. But the fans just keep buying and praying. In 2003, the Browns were 5-11, but online sales of Browns merchandise rose 67 percent, according to a story in the *Akron Beacon Journal* by Tom Reed. Overall, the Browns supposedly ranked 14th in the league, which is impressive given the dreadful state of the team. Granted, that's down from No. 3 when the team returned in 1999, but Browns fans still buying stuff in 2003 was remarkable. Just think what would happen if the team actually had a player whose jersey most fans wanted to wear!

As the 2004 season opened, the team was in the hands of Randy Lerner and Butch Davis. Al Lerner passed away in 2002. Policy resigned in the spring of 2004. The fans were angry, but still interested.

> I support the Browns for a few reasons. I have a complex that I like to support the underdog. I hate being a front-runner. I don't like people who are front-runners, who support a team for a while, then quiet down when it returns to its losing ways. I find myself asking, "Other teams have done it, why can't we?" It's comparable [to rooting for] the Chicago Cubs. I hold fast to the Browns despite the horrendous seasons.
>
> —Cody Wiewandt

Cody added that he's 14 years old.

If he likes underdogs, he sure picked the right team.

About the Author

Terry Pluto has been a sports columnist for the *Akron Beacon Journal* for more than 25 years. He has twice been nominated for a Pulitzer Prize and twice been honored by the Associated Press Sports Editors as the nation's top sports columnist for medium-sized newspapers. He is an eight-time winner of the Ohio Sports Writer of the Year award and has received more than 50 state and local writing awards. He is the author of 21 books, including *The Curse of Rocky Colavito* (selected by the *New York Times* as one of the five notable sports books of 1989), *Browns Town 1964*, and *Loose Balls*, which was ranked at number 13 on *Sports Illustrated's* list of the top 100 sports books of all time. He was called "Perhaps the best American writer of sports books," by the *Chicago Tribune* in 1997. He lives in Akron, Ohio.